Comprehensive
OFFICE PRACTICE

Alan Whitcomb
BA MEd PhD

Nelson

Acknowledgements

The author is particularly indebted to Mr P.E. Eustace for reading the manuscript draft and offering constructive criticisms of the work.

A.T.W.

Note to teachers

Teachers are invited to write to the author care of the publishers with any comments they wish to make on the suitability of this book for their purposes. Criticisms and suggestions for future editions will be gratefully received.

A.T.W.

Thomas Nelson and Sons Ltd
Nelson House   Mayfield Road
Walton-on-Thames   Surrey
KT12 5PL   UK

51 York Place
Edinburgh
EH1 3JD   UK

Thomas Nelson (Hong Kong) Ltd
Toppan Building 10/F
22A Westlands Road
Quarry Bay   Hong Kong

Thomas Nelson Australia
102 Dodds Street
South Melbourne
Victoria 3205   Australia

Nelson Canada
1120 Birchmount Road
Scarborough   Ontario
M1K 5G4   Canada

First published by Thomas Nelson and Sons Ltd 1983

ISBN 0-17-438178-6
NPN 9 8 7

Printed in Hong Kong.

Diagrams by KAG Design
Illustrations on pp1, 5, 8, 10, 14, 18, 20, 36, 39, 100, 101, 154 by Bob Wagner

Grateful acknowledgement for photographs and other copyright material are due to the following:

Alderman, Christopher pp 6, 100, 115, 116, 131
Barclays Bank Limited pp 86, 87, 88
Barnaby's Picture Library p 11
British Telecom pp 34, 35, 37, 39, 41, 42
Gestetner pp 133, 137, 141
H M Customs and Excise p 64
Inland Revenue p 162
Lewis, Barry (Network) p 15
Luncheon Vouchers Ltd p 14
Midland Bank Limited p 86
Royal Bank of Scotland pp 72, 73, 74, 75, 76, 77, 83, 84, 85, 86
The Post Office pp 44, 51, 52, 53, 91, 92, 93, 94, 95, 96, 97
Walmsley, John p 40
Watkins, Bob p 18

Cover photograph by John Sims

PREFACE

Offices today are changing very quickly because of the remarkable technological developments that are taking place, particularly those to do with the microprocessor. The widespread use of the latest microchip technology could eventually cost thousands of office jobs.

Fewer typists are likely to be needed in the future because the word processor has reduced the need for a typist to carry out much of the repetitive work.

For example, before the development of the word processor, legal documents, where often only top copies are acceptable, would perhaps have to be typed several times to produce just two perfect copies. These would then have to be checked against each other for mistakes to make sure they were identical. The word processor has changed all this. Now the typist only has to type the document once, and the word processor will type however many accurate top copies are required. Even spellings can be corrected, and paragraphs can be easily put in, taken out, or repositioned in seconds. Also, the completed text can be stored in the machine's memory on a magnetic tape or floppy disk and re-used or amended at a later date.

To be confident of work in the future the office worker will have to have many different skills and a knowledge of all aspects of business. This book, therefore, is concerned with the wide range of office activities in which they are likely to become involved.

Teachers will find that this text is suitable for students taking GCSE, RSA stages I and II, LCCI, PEI and similar level examinations. It will also be useful for students on BEC and SCOTBEC courses.

Students are also recommended to introduce themselves to the different forms of business which are dealt with in *Comprehensive Commerce*.

CONTENTS

1 INTRODUCTION TO THE OFFICE

The office is the centre of any business where there is a need to receive and send out communications, particularly those involved in the co-ordination of the different parts of the business. A well-organised office is an important part of any firm.

Why have an office?

- To organise and co-ordinate all action taken by the different parts of the business.
- To send and receive communication within the firm, and between the firm and other businesses.
- To keep records of all the activities that the business is involved in.
- To check and control money flow to make sure that funds are available to meet all costs.

Business organisation

Small firms

A small firm will obviously employ fewer people in its office than a large organisation. This often means that a person working in a small office will be involved in a greater number of activities. While this means that they will need to have more skills, it can make their work more interesting.

1

Large firms

A large firm is able to divide its workforce into divisions or departments, each of which may be large enough to have its own office. The diagram below shows a typical structure of a large company which manufactures and sells certain goods. There are, however, many other ways in which the structure might be organised.

Shareholders —————————— Board of Directors

Managing Director

company secretary	chief accountant	personnel manager	administrative officer	sales manager	chief buyer	production manager	transport manager
legal department	accounts department	personnel department	administration department	sales department	purchasing department	factory department	transport department

Look at this diagram. The shareholders of the business (the people who own the company) have elected a board of directors. This board decides on a general policy for running the company and appoints a Managing Director. The Managing Director's main responsibility is to make sure that the board's policy is followed and to oversee the day-to-day running of the company.

The firm has been divided into eight different departments. Each department has its own person in charge. The departments are as follows:

The legal department (company secretary)

This is the department which handles all the legal matters of the firm. For example, this department deals with: contracts, insurance, guarantees, compensation to employees, buying and selling of land, buildings and machinery.

The accounts department (chief accountant)

This important department is responsible for sending out invoices for goods or services provided by the firm and to see that bills sent by creditors (people who are owed money by the firm) are paid. This department will also check the overall financial situation of the company to make sure that it is not getting into financial trouble and that it is achieving satisfactory profits. The accounts department will often be responsible for paying the salaries and wages of the employees, although many companies will have a separate wages department.

The personnel department (personnel manager)

This department is sometimes called the staff department. It is responsible for the employment of new staff, which includes advertising for staff, contact with schools' careers teachers, interviewing and appointing staff. It also has the task of dismissing staff, and where necessary preparing references (often called testimonials) for anyone who is leaving the firm.

The personnel department looks after the general welfare of the employees and is often involved in encouraging and running the company's sports and social clubs. Some personnel departments include running a training school to provide training for new employees or for existing workers who need to learn new skills.

The administration department (administrative officer)

This is a general office which is mainly involved in the co-ordination of the activities of the different departments within the firm. It is usually to be found close to the main entrance and in this position it is well situated to be responsible for reception. Other duties covered by the department can include: the telephone services (the switchboard), the mail room, the internal supply of stationery and the running of a typing pool.

The sales department (sales manager)

The sales department is responsible for marketing the products or services that the company is selling. Where the firm is involved in overseas trade the department may be split into two: one department to handle home trade, and the other to deal with foreign trade.

Sometimes the sales office is responsible for the advertising and market research of the company, which involves making possible customers aware of the products or services being offered by the firm. However, often the business is large enough to form a separate advertising and market research department, or the firm may use an advertising agency to carry out this work for them.

The purchasing department (chief buyer)

The purchasing department is responsible for all items bought by the company. This might include purchasing machinery, raw materials for the factory to turn into finished goods, supplies of stationery or even food for the staff canteen. When invoices are received from suppliers they are checked by the purchasing department before being passed to the accounts department for payment.

The factory department (production/works manager)

Where a business is involved in manufacturing products this department is responsible for making sure that the goods are produced on time. The factory office may employ 'progress chasers'. These employees are responsible for two things: they will chase up parts and materials so that they will reach the production line on time and they will also check to make sure that the finished goods are not late in coming off the production line.

The transport department (transport manager)

Many large organisations will run their own fleet of vehicles to deliver the firm's produce to customers. Even when the company does not have its own vehicles, the transport manager's expert knowledge of this area makes it possible for them to choose the most appropriate method of transport. This knowledge is particularly valuable when goods have to be sent overseas because of the high costs involved.

Layout of the office

The layout of an office can consist of many enclosed small rooms linked by corridors (called an enclosed office) or a large open room with no partitions (called an open plan office). However, each of these layouts has its own disadvantages and to overcome these an office will often be a combination of both.

Enclosed offices

Advantages

- They offer privacy.
- They offer peace and quiet from the noise of machines and other employees.

Disadvantages

- They are expensive to build.
- They are difficult and expensive to rearrange.
- Building and rearranging such a layout requires detailed planning permission.
- Rooms in the middle of the building may not receive natural light.
- They can encourage slackness in employees because it is difficult to supervise their work.

An enclosed office   *An open plan office*

Open plan offices

Advantages

- They are cheap and easy to build.
- They are easy to rearrange and no planning permission is required.
- The whole floor space can receive natural light.
- They make it easier to supervise the employees.

Disadvantages

- There is a lack of privacy for confidential discussions.
- They can encourage idle chatter between employees.
- The noise from machines and employees can be disturbing.

One of the answers to the disadvantage of open plan offices lies in the use of acoustic screens (screens which reduce sound). These are free-standing screens which can be linked with other screens to form work areas. They can be bought in a variety of colours and textures, and acoustic (sound absorbing) padding inside the screens reduces noise levels. They can be simply rearranged at any time, and cost far less to move than the usual room divisions.

Working conditions

The Offices, Shops and Railways Premises Act, 1963

The general requirements of working conditions in the United Kingdom are laid down in this Act, a copy of which must be displayed in all offices.

This Act lays down several basic rules which must be obeyed by all employers. The main points covered by the Act which refer to offices are as follows:

- Cleanliness – offices must be kept clean.
- Lighting – offices should be well lit, either by natural or electric light.
- Comfort – a certain amount of floor space must be provided for workers and equipment (twelve square metres of floor space per person).
- Heating – the temperature must not fall below 16°C.
- Ventilation – offices should be well ventilated (i.e. there should be a good supply of fresh air and the offices should not become too stuffy).
- Toilets – must be provided with hot and cold running water, soap and clean towels.
- First aid – a first aid box should be provided and a number of staff trained in first aid.
- Safety – dangerous equipment and machinery should have shield devices, and electrical equipment should only be installed and repaired by qualified electricians.

The Contracts of Employment Act, 1972

More specific conditions of employment are set down in this Act. Employers have to give employees particulars of their main terms of employment, such as: job title, hours of work, holiday arrangements, legal rights and minimum periods of notice of employment. These terms of employment have to be set out in writing in a contract of employment. This must either be given to the employee or kept where he or she has access to it.

The Health and Safety at Work Act, 1974

This Act sets out employers' responsibilities concerning the health, safety and welfare of all employees. It covers the need to provide healthy working conditions and the arrangements which should be made for hazards such as fire. It also sets down rules for the maintenance and safety of machinery and equipment. However, the Act also states that every employee has a duty while at work to take reasonable care for the safety of themselves and other working colleagues.

Most firms recognise that good working conditions help to produce happy and efficient employees. They, therefore, try to provide working conditions which are better than those required by law.

WHAT DO YOU KNOW?

open plan offices
contract of employment
accounts department
enclosed offices
communications
departments
board of directors
company secretary
progress chasers
managing director

Write out all the following sentences filling in the missing words which you can choose from the list at the side of the test.

1 _____ are an important part of office activities.

2 Large businesses are able to divide their organisations into _____.

3 The _____ is elected by shareholders.

4 Day-to-day running of the firm is the responsibility of the _____.

5 The _____ is responsible for the legal office.

6 The _____ checks the overall financial situation of the company.

7 _____ are employed by the factory office to chase up supplies so that they will reach the production line on time.

8 _____ consist of many small and individual rooms.

9 _____ have the advantage that they are easy to rearrange.

10 Employers are required by law to set out in writing a _____ for each employee.

WHAT DO YOU KNOW?
continued

Answer the following questions by looking back at the text in this chapter.

1 Why have an office?

2 Copy the diagram showing the structure of a manufacturing company and write brief notes to explain the functions of each of the major departments.

3 Compare the advantages and disadvantages of enclosed and open plan offices.

4 How does the use of acoustic screens make open plan offices more acceptable?

5 What are the main features of each of the following Acts?
   a The Offices, Shops and Railways Premises Act, 1963
   b The Contracts of Employment Act, 1972

THINGS TO DO

There are a number of things in this picture which are against The Offices, Shops and Railways Premises Act, 1963. How many can you spot?

2 AN OFFICE JOB

There are a great variety of different jobs to be done in an office and in a large firm the type of job often depends on which department you are working for. For example, if you are working in the legal department you may well be typing contracts or dealing with insurance forms, and if you are in the accounts department you may well be dealing with invoices and bills, or perhaps wages and salaries. However, you may be working for the administration department in reception, dealing with visitors or working on the switchboard, or you may be working in the sales department typing up copy for advertisements.

Working in an office

Office juniors

The position of office junior is often the first office job given to a young person starting a career in office work. It involves carrying out all sorts of duties such as delivering messages, sorting and distributing mail, simple copy work such as addressing envelopes, filing, answering the telephone, and even making the tea for everyone else. At first sight it appears that the office junior is a 'slave' at everyone's beck and call. However, it introduces a new employee to the layout of the firm, its other staff and general office work. This provides useful training and a good grounding for promotion.

Clerical workers

Clerical workers, or 'clerks' as they are more commonly called, are people who carry out office work which cannot be done by machines alone. Their work includes record keeping, calculations, filing and handling written or telephoned customers' enquiries, and dealing with general correspondence.

Specialist office workers

Some workers may specialise in one particular area of office work. Examples of specialist clerical workers are employees who deal with just wages, or mail, or reprographics (duplicating and photocopying), or stock records. Some of these jobs require special training.

Typists

Typists may work for individuals in the firm, or they might be employed in a typing pool which brings together a number of typists in a separate department. In this department all typing is shared between the various typists.

Copy-typists These typists are involved in typing copies of information which has previously been written out, or filling in spaces on standard forms such as orders, invoices, credit and debit notes, quotations and contracts.

Audio-typists These typists have the task of typing correspondence from recordings made on dictating machines. To do this work the typist must have good spelling and knowledge of letter layout, paragraphing and punctuation.

Shorthand-typists These typists know how to write and transcribe shorthand. This job also requires a thorough knowledge of spelling, letter layout, paragraphing and punctuation. Often the shorthand typist will work for just one person, or perhaps a small group of, say, three or four people. The really good shorthand typist may be promoted to become a 'private' or 'personal' secretary to a senior executive.

The personal secretary is often involved in business meetings. They may organise them and sometimes take the minutes (notes) at them. In fact, this can be an important part of a personal secretary's job.

Business meetings

Any large business will organise meetings to communicate and discuss the general policy of the firm. These meetings may take the form of internal departmental meetings, meetings of the board of directors, or general meetings of the shareholders. Each of these types of meetings will have different business to discuss, but there are a few basic rules which should be followed.

While departmental or other internal meetings are usually informal, major meetings, such as the Annual General Meeting of a company, will be formal affairs. Such meetings as these should have a chairperson, a secretary and a treasurer:

- The chairperson will run the meeting, making sure that it is conducted in the proper manner and summing up all points discussed. The chairperson will also use their 'casting vote' when the meeting is equally divided on a point.
- The secretary is responsible for sending out notices of the meeting, preparing an agenda, recording the minutes and making sure that the decisions taken by the meeting are carried out.
- The treasurer is responsible for all financial matters and for maintaining financial records.

The agenda

The agenda is a list of what is to be discussed at the meeting and it is circulated to members before the meeting. It is usual for an agenda to contain the following items, which are numbered for convenience.

1 Apologies – received from those unable to be at the meeting.
2 Minutes – the minutes or notes made from the last meeting are read.
3 Matters arising (out of the minutes) – discussion and follow-up of matters or decisions taken at the last meeting.
4 Correspondence – important letters received since the last meeting.
5 Reports – may be made by the people who have special information to give to the meeting.
6 Special matters – here will be discussed the purpose of the present meeting. Decisions which have to be made, proposals to be discussed and voted on, action to be followed before next meeting.
7 Next meeting – date, time and place of next meeting.
8 Any other business (A.O.B.) – at this point members bring up points or questions not included in the agenda.

The minutes are a record of what takes place or is decided at each meeting. These may be just a summary of what has taken place, or a verbatim report, which means the main points of the meeting are repeated word for word.

Business meeting terms

Adjournment	With the approval of those present, the chairperson may adjourn the meeting. This means it will be continued at another time.
Amendment	A proposal to alter a motion by adding or deleting (getting rid of) words.
Motion	A motion is a formal proposal put forward by a member for discussion and voting upon at the meeting.
Nem. Con.	This means 'no one contradicting', i.e. no one has voted against the motion. However, some members may not have voted at all.
Quorum	This is the minimum number of persons who must be at the meeting before it can go ahead.
Resolution	A formal decision made at a meeting as a result of debate (discussion) and vote.

Applying for a job

When you are looking for a job you will often see that advertisements ask you to write in the 'first hand' or in the 'first instance'. This means that the prospective employer wishes to receive a hand-written letter of application. Such a letter should, of course, be neatly written, follow the correct method of layout (see Chapter 4) and care should be taken with spelling. The letter should give details of:

- Your previous employment, if you have been employed before.
- Qualifications, or examinations you are awaiting the result of.
- Your personal interests such as sports and social activities.
- A brief outline of why you are interested in obtaining the job you are applying for.

Sometimes, a job advertisement may ask applicants to send a 'curriculum vitae'. This means that the advertiser wishes you to provide a brief description of your life history and previous work experience. This may be written or typed on a separate sheet of paper.

From the various letters of application the company will draw up a short list of a few of the applicants (people who have applied for the job) whom they feel are the most suitable. The applicants on the short list will be sent a letter asking them to go for an interview. Along with this letter the applicant may be sent an application form to fill in. Again, this should be completed carefully and correctly.

CLERK TYPIST

This is an ideal opportunity for someone with initiative and enthusiasm to join the busy purchasing department of Sunhampton's foremost department store.

The job offers a good salary, 4 weeks' annual holiday and staff discount scheme. For an application form, write giving brief details of qualifications to:

The Personnel Manager
Floydds Ltd
High Street
Sunhampton

CURRICULUM VITAE

NAME Wendy Susan Jones

ADDRESS 24 Farmer Street, Bournemouth, BH2 6PX

NATIONALITY British

MARITAL STATUS Single

DATE OF BIRTH 24th December 1966

EDUCATION Blue Ridge Comprehensive School, Bournemouth (1978-1983)

QUALIFICATIONS (Awaiting examination results)

GCE O Level: English, Mathematics, Commerce, Geography

CSE: Typewriting, Office Practice, Computer Studies, German

EXPERIENCE One week of work experience at Hart Insurance Company, Bournemouth, dealing with incoming and outgoing mail and filing. Office Practice course at school involved operating the school reception desk. Saturday part-time work at Godfrey's Hardware Store, Bournemouth, dealing with customers and maintaining stock records.

HOBBIES Gardening, reading, music

OTHER INTERESTS Helping in day centre for old people

REFERENCES These may be obtained from:

The Headmaster, Blue Ridge Comprehensive School, Bournemouth

The Manager, Godfrey's Hardware Store, Bournemouth

APPLICATION FOR EMPLOYMENT

Surname *Jones* (Mr/Mrs/Ms)

Forename(s) *Wendy Susan*

Address *24 Farmer Street, Bournemouth BH2 6PX*

Nationality *British*   Date of birth *24/12/1966*

EDUCATION

School or College	Dates	Examinations taken
Blue Ridge Comprehensive School, Bournemouth	1978-83	GCE 'O' Levels: English, Mathematics Commerce, Geography CSE: Typewriting, Office Practice Computer Studies, German

PREVIOUS EMPLOYMENT

Name of employer	Dates	Position held
Godfrey's Hardware Store	1981 to present	Customers enquires and stock records clerk on Saturdays

Any other work experience

Office practice course operating school reception desk
one week at Hart Insurance Co. in post room and filing department

Hobbies and other interests

Gardening, reading, music
Helping in day centre for old people

Referees

Name *Dr S. Butterworth,*   Name *Mr H. Bracket,*
Position *Headmaster,*   Position *Manager,*
Address *Blue Ridge*   Address *Godfrey's Hardware Store,*
Comprehensive School,   *Bournemouth*
Bournemouth

Applicants signature *Wendy Jones*   Date *23/3/83*

OFFICE USE ONLY

Medical Report		School report References	
Date appointed	Department		Position

13

The interview

When you go for the interview you should take your examination result slips, your last school report if you have just left school, and any references (testimonials) you may have received from past employers.

The interview will probably take place in the personnel department and may be conducted by the personal manager, perhaps helped by the head of the department which you have applied to join. Many people are nervous when going for an interview, but the personnel manager will be aware of this and will do their best to put you at ease.

If the company decides you are the person they wish to employ they may well offer you the job at the interview. However, they may write to you formally to offer you the job. Whatever is the case, at the end of the interview you should know:

- what the job involves
- what the hours of work are
- what the holiday arrangements are
- what the wage or salary is
- what opportunities there are for promotion.

At the end of the interview the personnel manager is almost certain to ask if you have any questions. If you are not clear on any of the above points, this is the time when you should ask about them. At this point you should be prepared to tell the interviewer if you will accept the job if it is offered to you.

Terms of employment

When you are offered a job your employer will confirm:

- your wage or salary
- the time that you will be expected to arrive and leave work (hours of work)
- holiday arrangements
- any other benefits, such as Christmas bonus, pension schemes
- lunch arrangements.

Lunch arrangements

Some firms run their own canteen where food is often subsidised (partly paid for) by the company. Sometimes, however, the firm may give its employees luncheon vouchers. These are slips of paper, with various amounts of money printed on them, which are accepted in many restaurants and cafes as payment towards the cost of a meal. Some food shops also accept them.

Hours of work

Although some people work shift-work, most people work certain fixed hours, and, not surprisingly, most of them are going to and from work at similar times.

This system of working has the following disadvantages:

- It has large numbers of people trying to travel to and from work at the same time. This results in traffic jams and chaos on the trains and buses, especially on those travelling into cities and large towns.
- Public transport is not being used economically. This is because there are periods of over-use and there are periods of under-use.
- Not everybody finds it convenient to work the same hours as others. For example, the working mother may have to take young children to school before leaving for work.
- Workers need certain periods of time when they do not have to be at work during working hours. For example, they have to go to the bank, doctor, dentist or even the hairdresser.

It is also realised that in many businesses there are times when not all members of staff need to be present. At other busy 'core' times, everyone is needed at the same time.

Flexitime, and Flexible Working Time (FWT), are names used to describe a system which has been developed as an alternative to the usual one of working certain fixed hours.

What is FWT?

Flexitime is a system of arranging working hours so that at peak or core periods of work the maximum number of staff are available. Outside core time employees are able to choose the times they work by completing a required number of overall hours per week.

How does FWT work?

The working day of the firm is broken into three parts:

1 **Band time** This is the total period of time the business operates, for example, 8.00 a.m. to 6.00 p.m.
2 **Core time** This is the period of time when every member of staff is expected to work.
3 **Flexible time** This is the period outside the core time when an employee can choose whether they work or not, as long as during the week they work the total number of hours they are paid for.

Example:

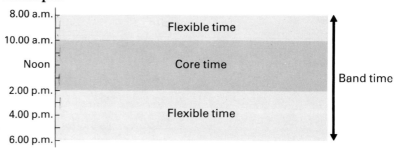

Total hours required by worker=35 hours.

To choose which hours to work the employee first calculates core time. Core time=5 days×4 hours (10.00 a.m. to 2.00 p.m.)=20 hours. This leaves 15 hours of working to choose from FWT. Before choosing the hours of flexitime the employee will have to take into account the time they wish to use for lunch breaks. Most firms will insist that a minimum of 30 minutes is taken for each lunch break.

WHAT DO YOU KNOW?

personnel department
first hand
flexible working time
clerks
quorum
luncheon vouchers
office junior
traditional working hours
minutes
agenda

Write out all the following sentences filling in the missing words which you can choose from the list at the side of the test.

1 The job of _____ introduces a new employee to the layout of the firm, its other staff and general office work.

2 _____ are people who carry out office work that cannot be done by machines alone.

3 The _____ is a summary of what is to be discussed at a meeting.

4 The _____ are a record of what takes place during a meeting.

5 A _____ is the minimum number of persons who must be at a meeting before it can go ahead.

6 If a job advertisement asks for applications in the _____ this means the letter should be handwritten.

7 Interviews for a job usually take place in the _____

8 _____ are slips of paper which are accepted in many restaurants as payment towards the cost of a meal.

9 A criticism of _____ is that it results in traffic jams at certain periods during the day.

10 With _____ workers have some choice in the hours they work.

Answer the following questions by looking back at the text in this chapter.

1 Give a brief description of the work of the various forms of typists.

2 What is an agenda and which items are contained in it?

3 How do ordinary minutes differ from a verbatim report?

4 Supposing you are interviewed for a job, what should you need to know by the end of the interview? How and when might the interviewer let you know if you have got the job?

THINGS TO DO

1 The following information is to be turned into an agenda for a meeting. Set it out as the example in this chapter.

'On the 20th of this month a meeting of the school parent-teacher association will take place. The meeting will be held in the school assembly hall at 3.00 p.m. The main item for discussion will be this year's visit to the school summer camp. Mr Eustace will report on a meeting he attended of the travel fund sub-committee. There should be an opportunity for members to discuss other business. The date and time of the next meeting has to be decided.'

2 What job would you like to do when you leave school or college? Look in a newspaper for advertisements to give you ideas.
   When you have found a job that you would like to apply for, write, or type, a curriculum vitae for yourself using the one in this chapter as an example.

3 Using the diagram of the FWT band time as an example, draw up a week's day-by-day work timetable for yourself, taking into account that you must work for 35 hours a week. Your employer also insists that you take a minimum of 30 minutes a day for lunch.

3 RECEPTION

The importance of the receptionist of a firm cannot be stressed enough. This is because she is often the first person that a visitor to the business meets.

Her work requires:

- a neat appearance
- a pleasant manner
- an ability to act with initiative and tact
- a thorough knowledge of the layout and personnel (staff) of the firm.

Where to find the receptionist

The receptionist is usually situated just inside the main entrance to the business. In a large firm a special reception area may be provided with a receptionist just to deal with visitors. In a smaller business it may be necessary for the receptionist to combine her work with other duties, and deal with visitors via an 'enquiries' window of her office. Some firms will use different people, who take it in turn for reception duties, to make sure that a number of employees have experience of meeting visitors.

The receptionist in a large firm may be helped in her duties by having messengers, or porters, who will work under her direction. These messengers may well take visitors to the people they wish to see once the receptionist has confirmed that it is in order to do so.

Reception areas will of course differ according to the size of the business, but many will have a buzzer or bell to call the receptionist when she is busy elsewhere. A telephone, and maybe a small switchboard or intercom, will be provided so that she can contact various parts of the firm to announce the arrival of visitors. Depending on the other duties of the receptionist, a typewriter may also be provided.

The reception area will be clearly signposted with the word 'reception' or 'enquiries'. It will have chairs and perhaps a small table with some magazines and possibly a few plants. These all help to make the visitor feel more comfortable while they are awaiting attention.

The work of the receptionist

Many receptionists will have an appointments book, in which will be noted the names of visitors who are expected at the firm and the time they are due to arrive. When the visitor arrives the receptionist will ask them to take a seat and contact the person they want to see. Having confirmed that the person is able to see the visitor, the receptionist will then take them to the person, or direct one of the messengers to do so.

Date: 1st July

Time	Management	Personnel	Accounts	Production	Marketing	Transport	Office Services	Purchases
9.00								
9.15	Mr Jones							
9.30								
9.45				Mr Black				
10.00								
10.15								
10.30		Ms Reed						
10.45								
11.00					Ms Osborn			
11.15								
11.30	Mr Green						Mr Lewis	
11.45								
12.00								
12.15		Mr Smith						
12.30								
12.45								
1.00								
1.15								
1.30								
1.45								
2.00	Ms Adams							
2.15								
2.30								Mr Evans

An appointments book

If the visitor does not have an appointment the receptionist must act with great tact. She should first ask for the caller's business card, who they wish to see and if they can briefly tell her what the visit is about.

The business card will show several things which will save some questions:

- the caller's name
- their company's name and address
- the position they hold within the company
- the type of business their firm is in.

Having found out why the visitor has come to the firm, the receptionist should ask them to sit down to wait, while she tries to contact the person they want to see. She might do this by using a radio pager, which calls the holder to the nearest telephone by bleeping, or, if possible, she will telephone the person direct. When telephoning the person the visitor wishes to see, the receptionist must again be tactful, especially if the caller is able to hear the telephone conversation.

Even if the person the visitor wants to see answers the telephone the receptionist should talk as if to some third person.

Example: A receptionist has telephoned through to the extension of Mr Carter, and it is Mr Carter who answers the telephone.

In handling the conversation in this way, it is easy for the receptionist to tell Mr Osborne that Mr Carter is not in the firm without offending him. If, however, the receptionist had said, 'Mr Osborne of Osborne Electronics is here to see you, Mr Carter. Can you see him?' the visitor would know that Mr Carter was in, and could be offended by a refusal to see him.

Many firms require a reception register to be kept by the receptionist to record the date and time of arrival and departure of visitors. This is especially important in companies where there is strict security.

Date	Name	Company	Address	Time of arrival	Referred to	Time of departure
23rd March	Mr Jones	Cat's Whisker Boutique	Swansea	9.15	Managing Director	10.30
"	Mr Black	Dislee Office Equip.	London	9.30	Production	9.45
"	Ms Reed	—	Local	10.00	Personnel	11.15
"	Ms Osborn	Osborn Advertising	Edinburgh	10.30	Marketing	11.45
"	Mr Lewis	Ellis Contracts	Local	11.00	Office Services	11.30

A reception register

The qualities of the receptionist

The good receptionist should:

- have a smart appearance
- have a pleasant manner
- enjoy meeting people
- be even-tempered and polite
- be discreet, and not disclose confidential information
- be tactful in handling unexpected visitors
- be able to act with initiative.

Additional work of the receptionist

Most receptionists will have other work to do in between dealing with visitors. The amount of additional tasks will largely depend on the size of the firm. The receptionist may be asked to operate a small switchboard (see Chapter 5), keep the petty cash record (see Chapter 6), or type letters and envelopes. She may, also, have to handle incoming and outgoing mail (see Chapter 6).

Almost certainly, the receptionist will at some time be involved in receiving letters, packages and parcels for which she will have to sign. However, she must not give her signature without careful consideration.

Some points to consider before signing for a parcel:

- Have the goods really been ordered by the firm? Check the official order number on the delivery note (see Chapter 7) or the name of the person who has ordered the goods.
- If the delivery note states three packages, are they all present? If not, write clearly on the delivery note the number of parcels actually delivered.
- Is the outer packaging damaged in any way? If so, write a description of the damage in addition to your signature.
- Is it possible to check that the goods are undamaged? If it is convenient to open the packages do so to check that the goods being delivered are undamaged and as stated on the delivery note.
- If it is inconvenient to look at the parcel contents add the words 'not examined' when signing.

WHAT DO YOU KNOW?

reception register
smart appearance
signature
appointments book
pleasant
'not examined'
messengers
business card
entrance
meeting people

Write out all the following sentences filling in the missing words which you can choose from the list at the side of the test.

1 The receptionist is usually situated near to the _____ of a business.

2 _____ or porters are sometimes employed to help the receptionist.

3 An _____ will be used to list expected callers.

4 A visitor's _____ can save a lot of questions.

5 Some firms require a _____ to be kept to record the date and the time that visitors arrive and depart.

6 A good receptionist should have a _____ manner.

7 A _____ is essential for a receptionist.

8 You will like reception work if you enjoy _____.

9 The receptionist should not give their _____ without careful consideration.

10 When signing for goods that you have been unable to inspect you should add the words _____.

Answer the following questions by looking back at the text in this chapter

1 Where is the receptionist situated in a firm, and why is their work so important?

2 Copy the example of an appointments book and explain the purpose of it.

3 Briefly describe how a receptionist should deal with a visitor who has an appointment.

4 Explain how a receptionist should deal with an unexpected visitor.

5 Make a list of the qualities of a good receptionist.

6 What work might someone be asked to do in addition to their work as a receptionist?

7 Why should careful consideration be given before signing for something delivered to your firm?

THINGS TO DO

Rule a reception register page, similar to the example in this chapter, and complete it for callers to your firm today.

9.15 a.m. Mr D. Batey, Sweyne Trading Co. Ltd.,
26 Eden Close, Colchester, Essex, CO2 9RT.
To see chief buyer. Left 9.45 a.m.

10.00 a.m. Ms Kerrie Wayne, 20 Podders Way,
Southend-on-Sea, Essex, SS1 3YX.
To see personnel manager. Left 11.30 a.m.

12.30 p.m. Mr C. Stone, Careers Teacher, Fodderwick School,
Colchester, Essex.
To see personnel manager. Left 1.15 p.m.

2.30 p.m. Mr P. Eustace, service mechanic,
Rendall Typewriter Services, Grays, Essex.
To see typing pool supervisor. Left 4.15 p.m.

Say why you think each of the last three visitors came to the firm.

4 BUSINESS CORRESPONDENCE

The transfer of messages from one person to another is referred to as communication. We are continually communicating with others, directly in conversation and indirectly by telephone or letter.

Successful communication requires:

- The sender of the message to make what they want to say clear and straightforward.
- The receiver to listen or read carefully, so that they do not misunderstand the message.

The business person will be concerned not only with making their message clear, but also in choosing between the various methods of communication available. The method they choose will depend on:

- Where they are, and what they are doing at the time they want to send the communication.
- The speed with which it is needed.
- The content of the message, for example, is it complicated or confidential?

In this chapter we will examine the basic forms of written communication used by people in business.

Letter writing

Letters which we write informally to our friends and relatives are called personal letters. Most letters sent out from offices are business letters. Sometimes it is also necessary for private individuals to write business or formal letters, for example, to their bank, local council, or in applying for a job. Therefore, it is important for everyone to know the correct way to write a formal letter.

Paper sizes

The standardised sizes of paper used today for letter writing are known as the International 'A' sizes – A0 A1 A2 A3 A4 A5 A6 A7. A0 is the largest of these sizes, whilst A7 is the smallest – A1 size equals half of A0, A2 is half of A1, A3 is half of A2, and so on.

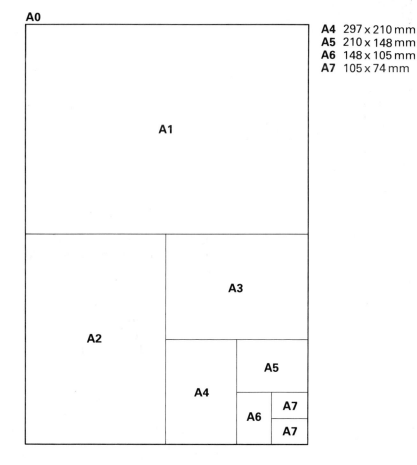

A4	297 x 210 mm
A5	210 x 148 mm
A6	148 x 105 mm
A7	105 x 74 mm

The sizes of paper most often used for letter writing in business are A4 and A5. The larger of these sizes, A4, measures 297mm × 210mm. A5 paper (half of the size of A4) measures 210mm × 148mm.

Paper is usually sold by the ream. There are 500 sheets of paper in a ream.

Parts of a business letter

A business letter can be divided into parts.

a Letter heading

Business letters usually have a printed heading which includes the:

- name of the firm
- type of business
- address and telephone number
- telex number (if available)
- names of directors, company secretary, chairperson
- words: 'Our ref.' and 'Your ref.'

b Reference

Reference numbers are useful in helping to identify a particular letter. A letter may show the reference number of the person to whom the letter is being sent, if known, as well as the reference of the sender.

There are many methods of arranging references. Often they will consist of the initials of the dictator, the typist and the number of the letter. Sometimes, the reference may include the name of the department from which the letter has been sent.
For example, ATW/SO   ATW/SO/12   CLAIMS/SO/12.

c Date

The date shown is the date the letter is sent. This can be shown as: '20 June 198—' or 'June 20, 198—'.

d Name and address of addressee

The addressee is the person to whom the letter is being sent. All lines should begin at the margin:

Mr A. MacDonald,
27 Hyde Park,
ABERDEEN,
AB2 7ZR

e Salutation

The salutation is the opening words of greeting which begin the letter. For example,

Dear Sir, Dear Sirs, Dear Madam, Dear Mr James, Dear Peter.

f Subject headings

The main subject or topic of the letter can be used as a brief heading immediately below the salutation. This allows the receiver of the letter to know what it is about at a glance:

Dear Sirs,

Office Practice Examination

a AKELA HARDWARE COMPANY LIMITED
9 SMITH STREET, BLANDFORD FORUM, DORSET DT11 7FX Telephone: Blandford 4282

Directors: David Anderson (Managing), Peter Lloyd, Ann Williams, Robert Wood

```
        Our Ref.   DA/HL/64
b       Your Ref.  JB/KW/N9

c       12th June 1983

d       Mr T. Watson,
        Messrs Walker Trading Ltd,
        5 Stanbridge Way,
        Colbrook,
        SLOUGH, SL3 6PP

e       Dear Mr Watson,

f                           Order number G3246

g       We thank you for your order number G3246 dated 6th June,
        for 12 'Seacrest' bathroom suites.  This order will be
        despatched in accordance with your instructions within
        two weeks.

        We should like to bring to your attention the new range
        of suites we shall be offering from the end of next month.
        In this respect we take the liberty of enclosing our leaflets
        for the new range.

        The colour chart for the new line is not available for
        another week, but may we suggest that our representative
        could bring this to you the next time he is in your area.

h       Yours sincerely,
        AKELA HARDWARE COMPANY LIMITED

i       David Anderson

        David Anderson
        (Managing Director)

j       Encs.
```

g Body of the letter

This part of the letter contains the message or information that the sender wishes to pass to the addressee.

- **Introduction** This paragraph refers to any previous correspondence and outlines the business of the letter.
- **Main points** This paragraph states clearly the points you wish to make. Do not assume that the reader will know anything about the points that you wish to make.
- **Conclusion** This paragraph suggests what future action (if any) you think should follow your letter.

h Complimentary close

This is the method used to close the letter. The most common forms used today are: 'Yours faithfully' and 'Yours sincerely' (note small 'f' and 's').

The choice of complimentary close depends on the salutation used.

Salutation	*Complimentary Close*
Dear Sir,	Yours faithfully,
Dear Sirs,	Yours faithfully,
Dear Madam,	Yours faithfully,
Dear Mr James,	Yours sincerely,
Dear Peter,	Yours sincerely,

Many companies include typing the company's name in capitals immediately below the complimentary close.

i Signature

The signature of the person who is sending the letter will be written below the complimentary close, and the company name if typed. This may be followed by the person's name and the position held in the company.

Yours faithfully,
LEGG ENTERPRISES LTD

John Langley

JOHN LANGLEY
(Managing Director)

j Enclosures

When something is sent with the letter, for example, a brochure, attention is drawn to it by typing the word 'Enclosure', 'Enc.' or 'Encs.', at the bottom left-hand corner of the letter.

Checklist for letters

- Is the letter complete?
- Does it clearly state what you want to say in a way that will not be misunderstood by the receiver of the letter?
- Are the following correct: spelling, punctuation, address, salutation, complimentary close?
- Has the letter been signed?
- If there are any enclosures, are they indicated and present?
- Is the envelope address the same as the inside address?

Internal correspondence

Memoranda

A standard form, known as a memorandum or memo, is used for internal communication between members of a firm. No salutation or complimentary close is necessary and the messages tend to be brief and to the point.

MEMORANDUM

To Purchasing Department

From Sales Office   Date 13 February 1983

Subject Sales Invoices - Requisition 3158, 2 January

We have not yet received the sales invoices we asked you to place on order for us, although your acknowledgement note indicated that the delivery date was last Monday.

Our supply of sales invoices is now very low. Please telephone your supplier and ask them to carry out delivery.

MEMORANDUM

To Purchasing Department

From Sales Office   Date 13 February 1983

Message	Reply
Sales Invoices Requisition 3158 2 January	We have contacted supplier who tell us that delivery will be made direct to your office before 5.00 p.m. this afternoon.
We have not yet received the sales invoices we asked you to place on order for us, although your acknowledgement note indicated that delivery date was last Monday.	
Our supply of sales invoices is now very low. Please telephone your suppliers and ask them to carry out delivery.	

Memos can have a space for a reply

Sometimes memos, or even incoming mail, journals and catalogues need to be seen by more than one person, and there are various ways this can be arranged.

Circulation slips

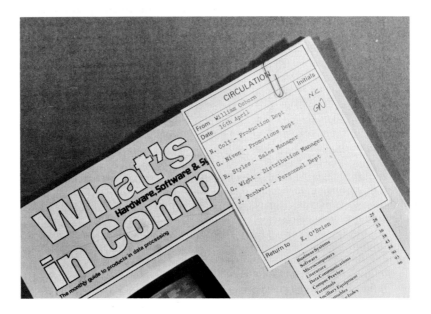

A circulation slip can be attached to the communication. This slip bears the names of the people or departments that need to see the communication. After each person has seen it they pass it on to the next person on the list.

Distribution stamp

An alternative to the circulation slip is the distribution stamp. This is a rubber stamp which is used to stamp a circulation list on to a document. This circulation list is similar to that shown on the circulation slip.

Routing slip

A routing slip is another method of sending documents round to various members of a firm. This slip is numbered to show the order in which members of the firm are to see the document.

ROUTING SLIP		
Please initial and circulate quickly in the order shown		
3	L. Carter	LC
1	P. Eustace	PE.
2	H. Letchford	HL
5	M. Perry	
4	A. Whitcomb	AW
6	D. Woolard*	
	* for filing	

Correction signs and abbreviations

It is important to remember that you must never send a letter or memo with a mistake in it. If mistakes have been made in a letter they may well be corrected by using some of the signs below. The letter must then be retyped.

Correction	Sign in margin	Sign in text
Insert full stop	⊙/	⅄
Insert comma	⁊	⅄
Insert question mark	?/	⅄
Insert apostrophe	⁊	⅄
Use capital letters	Caps/	≡
Insert word(s)	Words/	⅄
Use italics	ital/	————
Use lower case letters	l.c./	encircle letter(s)
Transpose (to change the order of) words or letters	trs/	⌐⌐
Delete (get rid of)	⁊	letters crossed out
To remain as it was	stet/	dotted line under words wrongly struck through
Space required	#/	⅄
Close up the space	⌒/	⌒
Start a new paragraph	N.P./	⌐

Some useful business abbreviations

a/c, acc., acct	account		f.o.c.	free of charge
a.s.a.p.	as soon as possible		f.o.r.	free on rail
@	at		G.P.	general practitioner
bal.	balance		H.M.S.O.	Her Majesty's Stationery Office
b/d	brought down		H.P.	hire purchase
b/f	brought forward		H.Q.	headquarters
B/S	balance sheet		i.e.	that is
cap(s)	capital letter(s)		inst.	instant, current month
c/d	carried down		J.P.	Justice of the Peace
c/f	carried forward		Jr, Jun., Junr	Junior
c.f.	cost and freight		l.c.	lower case
C/N	credit note		Ltd	limited liability
Co.	Company		memo	memorandum
c/o	care of		O.H.M.S.	On Her Majesty's Service
C.O.D.	cash on delivery		P.A.Y.E.	Pay As You Earn
Cr.	credit or creditor		PLC	Public Limited Company
CWO	cash with order		p.p.	pages, *per pro* (for and on behalf of)
dept	department		P.P.	parcel post
do., ditto	the same		R/D	refer to drawer
D/N	debit note		re	with reference to
Dr	debtor, Doctor		ref.	reference
E.E.C.	European Economic Community		S.A.Y.E.	Save As You Earn
E.F.T.A.	European Free Trade Association		sen., senr	senior
e.g.	for example		sgn.	signed
E & OE	errors and omissions excepted		stet	let it stand
Enc., Encl.	enclosure		u.c.	upper case
Esq.	Esquire		v.	versus, against
f.o.b.	free on board		VDU	visual display unit

WHAT DO YOU KNOW?

yours faithfully
half
communication
p.p.
business letters
clear
memos
ream
salutation
personal letters

Write out all the following sentences filling in the missing words which you can choose from the list at the side of the test.

1 The term _____ refers to the transmission of messages.

2 Successful communication requires the sender of the message to make what he or she wants to say as _____ as possible.

3 We write _____ to our friends.

4 Letters sent out from offices are _____.

5 A5 size paper is _____ the size of A4.

6 Paper is usually sold by the _____.

7 The _____ is the opening words of a letter.

8 A salutation of 'Dear Sir', requires a complimentary close of
_____.

9 For internal communications between members of a firm
_____ are used.

10 The abbreviation _____ stands for 'per pro' (for and on
behalf of).

Answer the following questions by looking back at the text in this
chapter.

1 What is necessary for successful communications?

2 Explain the difference between personal and business letters.

3 With the aid of a simple diagram explain the International 'A'
sizes of paper.

4 Describe the main parts of a letter and their positioning on a
sheet of A4-size writing paper.

5 What tips would you give to someone to help them write a
business letter?

6 What is the purpose of a memorandum and how does it differ
from a letter?

7 Produce diagrams of a circulation slip and a routing slip. How
do they differ from each other?

THINGS TO DO

Look at this short extract from a letter. Note that ten mistakes
have been made and corrected. Now rewrite or retype it including
the corrections. When you have finished, check to see if you have
corrected it properly by turning to the letter on page 27.

#/ trs/ 'We should like to bring to your attention the new ranged of ∘/
stet/ lc./ suites we shall be offering from the end of next Month. in this Cap /
we/ trs/ respect take the liberty fo enclosing our leaflets for the new ∘/
∘/ range.'

5 TELECOMMUNICATIONS

Making laser chips in a gold-lined furnace at Martlesham research laboratories. Laser technology is central to the use of optical fibres – hair-thin strands of glass that carry signals in the form of pulses of light. A pair of fibres can carry almost 2,000 simultaneous calls and by 1990 there will be 100,000km of optical fibre in the British TELECOM network, with 50 per cent of all long-distance traffic carried by light.

This light easy-to-handle coil of optical fibre cable can carry the same number of calls as the conventional coaxial cable on the drum in the background. Optical fibre cable is less expensive to manufacture and install and carries signals over long distances with little attenuation, distortion or cross talk interference.

Prestel – the world's first public viewdata system – links TV sets to computers by telephone to bring updated and virtually unlimited information into offices and homes. Viewers can use Prestel to make hotel or airline bookings, buy goods and services with credit cards, or send messages to other users.

Cardphones which accept plastic cards instead of cash are in British railway stations, airports and city centres. When it is inserted a visual display shows the amount of credit remaining. Cards containing either 40 or 200 units can be purchased in advance from post offices or from designated shops.

It has become increasingly important for businesses to be able to pass or exchange messages immediately.

One of the major suppliers of services which pass information in this way is British Telecom. There are, however, also other private companies which compete with British Telecom to supply these services.

The telephone

This service has now become an essential part of any business, especially since the introduction of the Subscriber Trunk Dialling (S.T.D.) system has meant that a person can contact most parts of the United Kingdom, and indeed, most parts of the world, in just a matter of seconds.

Before S.T.D. was introduced the telephone subscriber (the person who rents a telephone) could dial local calls, but had to go through a telephone exchange when they wanted to make a trunk (long distance) call. This was to allow the telephone operator to make the connection with the other number. Now, by use of the S.T.D. system, a subscriber can dial the code number of the area that they wish to contact and then the number of the subscriber that they wish to speak to, and the connection is made automatically. The service of operator connection is still available, but it carries a special charge.

Another telephone service which is available, and of particular use to people in business, is the radio telephone. In some areas of the United Kingdom it is possible to buy a radio telephone which will accept calls to and from any other telephone within the country. Calls can also be made to, although not received from, many countries abroad. The mobile radio equipment for this means that a person can have a telephone in their car, or even on their boat. However, the equipment must be bought from a manufacturer who has been approved by British Telecom.

The telephone switchboard

Many businesses today have a number of telephone extensions within the company. These telephones will probably be connected to one switchboard. If the switchboard is a Private Manual Branch Exchange (PMBX) it will need a switchboard operator to connect all the calls, whether incoming, outgoing or internal (from one extension to another). However, if a Private Automatic Branch Exchange (PABX) is used a switchboard operator need only connect the incoming calls. To make an outgoing call a person will just dial a special number (usually 9) to get an outside line and then dial in the normal way, and an internal call will be dialled direct and connected automatically by the switchboard.

Whichever switchboard is used, the switchboard operator is of special importance to the firm because it is their voice that the caller first hears, and the impression that the operator gives while handling the call can be very important to the success of the business. Indeed, any person who has to answer the telephone needs to follow the rule of three Ps:

Patient – they need to keep their temper and be understanding even though callers may, at times, be rude or slow to come to the point.
Pleasant – they need to be polite, but not over familiar.
Precise – they need to keep conversation clear and to the point.

Telephone tips

Receiving calls

- Answer calls promptly
- Give your number, name and organisation
- Keep coming back to waiting callers
- Speak clearly and politely at all times
- Don't be over familiar
- Keep a message pad handy
- If you cut a caller off, telephone them back

Making calls

- Make a note of points you want to ask beforehand
- Dial the correct number carefully
- Give your name and organisation
- State the name of the person you wish to speak to, or briefly state the purpose of your call so that you can be put through to someone who can help you.

WRONG	RIGHT
'Hello'	Give the name of your firm or department
'Who's that?'	'Who is calling, please?'
'Who do you want?'	'Who do you wish to speak to?'
'What did you say your name is?'	'Would you repeat your name, please?'
'He's not in.'	'I'm sorry the person you wish to speak to is not here at present. Can I help you or get him to phone you back?'
'Hold on.' 'Hang on a minute.'	'Would you hold the line, please?'
'Right ho.' 'O.K.'	'Yes, certainly.'

The telephone alphabet

In order to avoid misunderstanding in the spelling of difficult words over the telephone, British Telecom recommend the use of the 'telephone alphabet'. This substitutes names for letters to help spell out words.

A	Alfred	J	Jack	S	Samuel
B	Benjamin	K	King	T	Tommy
C	Charlie	L	London	U	Uncle
D	David	M	Mary	V	Victor
E	Edward	N	Nellie	W	William
F	Frederick	O	Oliver	X	X-ray
G	George	P	Peter	Y	Yellow
H	Harry	Q	Queen	Z	Zebra
I	Isaac	R	Robert		

Telephone Message

Date: 6 December   Time: 2·15 pm
Caller's name: Ronald Watt
Tel. no. Seagry 0254   Ext. no. 15

Message for: Helen Holliday
Message:

Mr Watt is unable to make the appointment on December 10th

Could you phone to arrange another time?

Received by: John Driscoll

The telephone message pad

It is common today for firms to provide their employees with printed pads for writing down telephone messages. These pads help to make sure that messages are not forgotten, and the printed sections of the message sheet remind each person to put down all the important information.

Telephone answering machine

There are a variety of machines which will answer the telephone and record a message for the owner when they are not in the office. The owner of the machine can then play back the recording on their return.

A telephone answering machine is connected to the telephone lines. When an incoming call is received, the machine will answer the call with a pre-record message, and the caller will then give his message which will be recorded.

Useful reference books for the telephone user

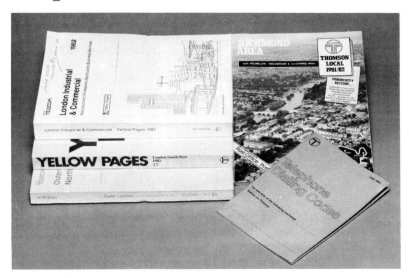

Telephone directories

These are issued free to subscribers. They contain names, addresses and telephone numbers of most people and firms who have telephones. Directories for areas other than the subscriber's own can be bought.

Some people, for various reasons, do not like to have their telephone number known publicly and do not have them entered in the directory. Such numbers are known as 'ex-directory' numbers and can only be obtained from the subscribers themselves.

Classified directories (yellow pages)

These directories are also issued free to telephone subscribers. They list free of charge names, addresses and telephone numbers of all business subscribers. Displayed and bold face entries may be included, but there is a charge for this. The names are listed in alphabetical order in respect of the trade offered:

    cleaning
    driving schools
    restaurants

The dialling code booklet

This is issued free to all subscribers. It lists all exchanges which can be dialled, giving codes and charges. It also gives you advice on how to get the best from your telephone, and information about the various telephone services, such as the recorded information services, including dial a disc, the weather forecast, the time and motoring information.

Other telephone services

Advice of duration and charge (ADC)

For a small fee, the telephone operator will time a call that has been connected by them and will advise you how long it lasted and how much it cost.

Personal calls

It is possible to make a call, through the operator, requesting to speak to a particular person. The charge for this call does not begin until the requested person is reached. However, a small charge is made even if the person is not available.

Alarm calls

It is possible to arrange for the telephone exchange operator to ring a particular telephone number at a certain time, for example, early in the morning.

Freefone

A subscriber can rent a Freefone number which means that they pay for any calls rather than the callers. This service is used mostly by traders wishing to encourage possible customers to contact them.

Telephone credit cards

This card allows a telephone subscriber to make a call from any telephone in this country or abroad and have the call charged to their own telephone bill. To use this service, the subscriber makes an operator connected call and quotes the number shown on their credit card. A quarterly charge is made for the card and the cost of the operator connected call is higher than a STD call. This service, however, is particularly useful to the person who travels a great deal in their work and who frequently needs to contact their office by using public telephones.

Transferred charge calls (or reversed charge)

The caller may pass the cost of an operator connected call to the account of the subscriber receiving the call, providing the subscriber agrees to accept the charge. This charge is higher than normal.

Green pages

These are usually included in the telephone directory and contain information that every telephone customer should know, for example, the services available and how to obtain them.

The telex service

Although the telephone is important and useful to the person in business, it does have one big disadvantage. This disadvantage is that the communications are not in printed form. Sometimes it is necessary to pass complicated information from one person to another very quickly. If we use the telephone for this kind of message it is possible that it may not be recorded correctly.

The telex service, however, provides immediate transfer of messages in printed form, and therefore reduces the risk of mistakes. Messages can be sent to subscribers in the United Kingdom and many overseas countries.

Subscribers to the telex service rent a machine called a teleprinter, which looks in many ways, like a combination between a typewriter and a telephone, with a keyboard, paper feed and a dial.

Each subscriber is issued with a telex number which is listed in a telex directory. Contact with another subscriber is made by dialling their telex number. If their machine is available to

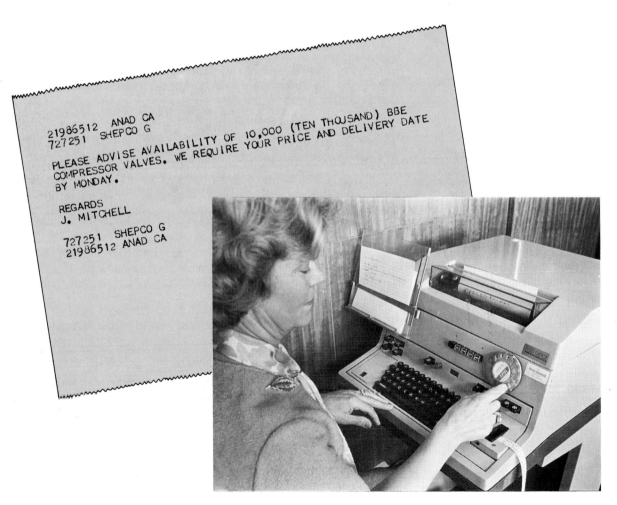

receive messages a green light appears on the sender's teleprinter. If the receiver is engaged a red light appears.

When connection is made between two teleprinters the operator types the message and it is automatically printed out on the receiving machine.

It is also possible to send messages using punched tape. This saves time if the receiver is engaged. The operator can prepare a punch tape by using a special piece of equipment which can be attached to the teleprinter. The machine will then automatically dial out the required number and transmit the message when the receiving machine is available.

A particular advantage of the telex service is that it is not necessary for someone to be present to receive messages. As long as a teleprinter is left switched on it will take down messages.

Teletex

The British Telecom Teletex Service allows the business person to send an A4 page of text in less than 10 seconds.

The letter, or whatever is to be sent, is typed on a machine called a terminal which then transmits it to one or several receiving terminals, thus reducing paper handling and delays.

Each Teletex terminal has its own identity number issued by British Telecom. The terminal will transmit a message only when it has confirmed the identity of the called terminal. Users can even adopt 'passwords' for additional security.

When the letter arrives at its destination it is stored electronically and can be printed at the receiver's convenience. The stored letter may even be displayed on a television-like screen.

The aim is to eventually make this a world-wide service.

Warning: Do not confuse 'Teletex' with 'Teletext'. 'Teletex' is communication via electronic text terminals. 'Teletext' refers to the Ceefax and Oracle services provided by the broadcasting authorities.

Bureaufax

British Telecom also provides a service whereby a black and white document, or photograph, up to A4 in size can be fed into a special machine and a copy of it is immediately transmitted to another machine. The receiving machine can be somewhere else in the United Kingdom or even abroad. These machines are called transmission machines.

Customers can buy their own transmission machines or they can use the Bureaufax service which is available at counter acceptance offices in many major towns and cities.

The Confravision service

Imagine the difficulties involved for people who have to attend a conference where they must meet many other executives from different parts of the country.

They have to:

- travel many miles to get to the conference
- face the hazards of fog, frost, snow and unreliable transport
- arrange overnight accommodation.

This obviously takes up a great deal of time and is expensive. British Telecom provides a Confravision service which allows people to hold face-to-face discussions, but without the inconvenience of everyone travelling to the same meeting place.

The Confravision service provides studios in cities throughout the United Kingdom, which link up by sound and vision, so that discussions can take place as if all those attending the meeting were present in the same room.

WHAT DO YOU KNOW?

Bureaufax
STD
· telex
Confravision
PABX
teleprinter
telephone alphabet
· yellow pages
PMBX
· answering machine

Write out all the following sentences filling in the missing words which you can choose from the list at the side of the text.

1 By use of _____ a telephone subscriber can dial another subscriber direct.

2 With a _____ an internal telephone system needs an operator.

3 A _____ provides automatic transfer of calls within a business.

4 The _____ is used to substitute names for letters in the spelling of difficult words over the telephone.

5 A telephone _____ will record messages.

6 The _____ lists traders who are telephone subscribers.

7 The _____ service provides immediate transfer of printed messages.

8 The telex service uses a machine called a _____.

9 An exact copy of a photograph or document can be transmitted instantly using the _____ service.

10 The _____ service links business people by both sound and vision.

Answer the following questions by looking back at the text in this chapter.

1 Explain what the Subscriber Trunk Dialling system is and its advantages over previous systems.

2 What is the difference between a PMBX and a PABX?

3 What rules and tips would you offer anyone who has to answer the telephone on behalf of a firm?

4 Copy out the telephone alphabet. How would you spell out your own Christian name using the alphabet? Write it down.

5 Explain the purpose of the telephone answering machine.

6 What advantages has the telex service got over the telephone?

7 Give a brief description of the Confravision service.

8 Describe the British Telecom Teletex and Bureaufax services.

THINGS TO DO

1 Read the green pages and the dialling code book and make brief notes about the various recorded services available, such as bedtime stories, dial a disc etc.

2 Read the green pages and write brief notes about the various telephone equipment that is illustrated.

3 From the green pages and the dialling code book, explain how one might make an international call.

6 THE MAIL ROOM

An important part of the communications system of a business is the support given by the mail room (sometimes called the post room) of the firm. This department handles incoming and outgoing mail.

Incoming mail

When mail is received, the staff of the mail department will first of all separate envelopes which are marked for the 'personal' or 'confidential' attention of members of the firm. These are distributed unopened to the people to whom they are addressed, or to their personal secretaries.

The rest of the mail is carefully opened with a letter knife or an electric letter-opener. Care is taken to make sure that nothing is left in the envelopes. Some firms even keep envelopes for a few days, in case anything has been left in them by mistake.

Any enclosures are attached to the front of the letter that goes with them. In attaching any enclosures, care must be taken to make sure that no damage is done to any documents.

The rule of typing 'Enc.' or 'Enclosure' at the bottom of a letter to show that something is enclosed, is useful for the receiver as it tells them to look out for it. However, should an enclosure be indicated and not found, the words 'Not Enclosed' should be written on the letter beside the word 'Enclosure'.

The mail should now be stamped with a date stamp before being distributed to the various people or departments. The date stamp is useful for checking against if there is later some query of

An electric letter-opener

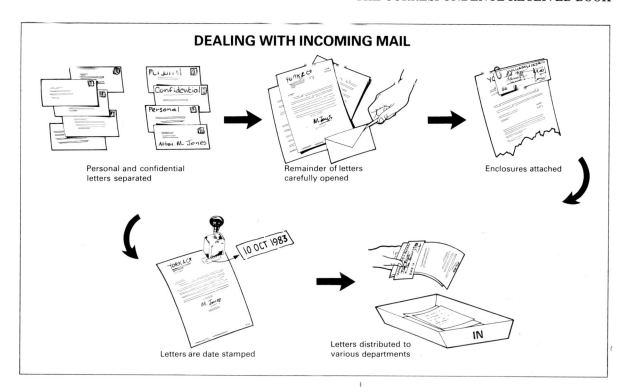

DEALING WITH INCOMING MAIL

Personal and confidential letters separated

Remainder of letters carefully opened

Enclosures attached

Letters are date stamped

Letters distributed to various departments

IN

delay in dealing with a letter. However, care must be taken in stamping the letters so that the stamp does not cover up some important information. It should be placed where nothing is written. If necessary, it should be printed on the reverse of the letter.

Simple though it may seem, the sorting and distribution of mail is a task that requires a good deal of skill. It requires the mail room staff to have a thorough knowledge of the firm, and all its employees, and to be well organised so that they can distribute the mail as quickly as possible.

The correspondence received book

Some firms use a correspondence received book (sometimes called the incoming mail register) to record mail as it is distributed to the various members of the firm. This book records when, and to which department, each letter is passed.

Some correspondence received books also record who replies to each letter

Letter from	Dated	Received	Passed To	Reply by	Date
B. Carter	1-9-83	2-9-83	Advertising	K. Durant	3-9-83
J. Ware	1-9-83	2-9-83	Buying	A. Smith	3-9-83
H. Black	2-9-83	4-9-83	Production	R. James	6-9-83
P. Eustace	2-9-83	7-9-83	Sales	J. Chapman	8-9-83

The remittance record book

Another useful record book used by some mail rooms is the remittance record book. When letters are received enclosing remittances, such as cheques, postal orders or cash, they are recorded in this book before being passed to the cashiers.

Letter from	Dated	Received	Amount	Cashiers	Date
W. Vine	5-9-83	6-9-83	£1,100-00	ALP	6-9-83
White Bros	6-9-83	8-9-83	£ 25-60	ALP	8-9-83
Brown & Co.	6-9-83	8-9-83	£ 350-25	ALP	8-9-83
L.C.R.	7-9-83	8-9-83	£ 200-10	ALP	8-9-83

Outgoing mail

Some firms arrange for each individual department to be responsible for the sealing of their own mail, which is then passed to the mail room for posting. Other firms will want signed letters and their envelopes passed to the mail room where they will be folded and sealed ready for posting. In either case, make sure that:

- The letters are checked to see if they have been signed, and enclosures included where necessary.
- The envelope address is checked against the name and address shown on the letter to go inside.

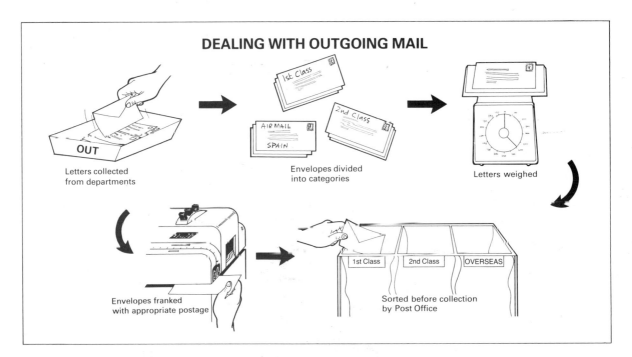

DEALING WITH OUTGOING MAIL

OUT
Letters collected from departments

1st Class
AIR MAIL SPAIN
2nd Class
Envelopes divided into categories

Letters weighed

Envelopes franked with appropriate postage

1st Class | 2nd Class | OVERSEAS
Sorted before collection by Post Office

- The letters are folded and put into the envelopes. Care must be taken in folding letters so that unnecessary creases are not made in them.
- The envelopes are sealed. This may be done by using a roller with a water reservoir, although a large firm with many envelopes to seal, may use an envelope sealing machine.

Postage stamps are stuck on to the letters and packages after they have been weighed so that the correct postage is shown. The rate of postage will vary, depending on the weight of the package and the current charge made by the Post Office. The rate of postage can be looked up in the current Post Office Guide, but it is better if the rates are displayed in the post room. This saves the trouble of having to keep referring to the Post Office Guide.

Post Office Preferred envelopes

Since 1966 the Post Office has asked all its customers to post their mail in Post Office Preferred (POP) envelopes. The use of POP envelopes helps the Post Office in its mechanised handling of mail. Eventually, a higher rate of postage will be charged for envelopes that are not POP.

To come within the POP range, envelopes should be at least 90 mm×140 mm and not larger than 120 mm×235 mm. They should be oblong in shape and made from paper weighing at least 63 grammes per square metre. Similar regulations also apply to the size and shape of postcards.

The franking machine

If a firm has a large amount of mail to send out, sticking stamps on to the envelopes and packages can take up a great deal of time. The time taken to do this task can be considerably speeded up by the use of a franking machine or postage meter.

A franking machine can be hired or purchased from companies which are authorised by the Post Office. The user of a franking

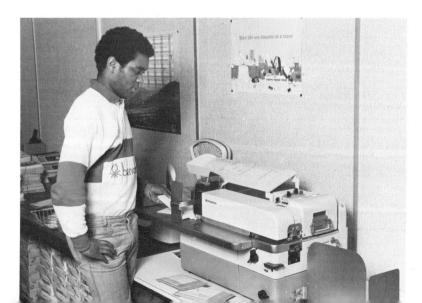

machine pays a sum of money to the Post Office in pre-payment of postage, and the meters on the machine are set to that amount, say, £200. The machine can be set to produce varying postage amounts, and it will print these amounts on the envelopes. At the same time it also prints 'postage paid', the date, place of posting and the die number of the machine. Each machine has a different number, which is known as its die number. The machine can also be set to print an advertising slogan as well as the postage.

Slips of gummed paper, about 25 millimetres wide, can be franked for fixing to parcels which are too big to pass through the machine.

As the amounts of postage are issued by the machine it registers the amount of used and unused postage, and reduces the metered pre-payment accordingly. At the end of each week, a weekly control card must be passed to the Post Office stating the number of units used. The firm must pay for further meter units when they begin to run low.

The postage book

At one time all businesses would keep a record of all money spent on postage in a postage record book. Today, the use of the franking machine has made this unnecessary, but some firms, for example, those not using a franking machine, still require a record of postage.

There are different methods of recording postage details, but a typical example would show the date of despatch (posting), the name of the person or firm to whom the letter is sent, their address (perhaps abbreviated) and the amount of postage.

Two different ways of recording postage details in a postage book

Received	Date	Name & Address	Postage	
£	1983		£	p
10.00	Oct 14	Brown Bros, London		20
	Oct 14	Bishops Ltd, Liverpool		15
	Oct 14	J. Roberts, Birmingham	1	15
	Oct 14	E. Jones, Cardiff		20

Received	Date	Description	Postage	
£	1983		£	p
10.00	Oct 14	Letters	1	30
	Oct 14	Parcels	1	15
	Oct 14	Circulars		80
	Oct 15	Letters	1	10

Petty cash (imprest system)

The amount spent on postage, and many other petty (small) amounts of business expenditure, are recorded by the petty cash cashier who is often also the postal clerk. The most common system which is used to record the petty cash expenditure is called the imprest system.

This system means that a set amount of cash, say £20, is advanced by the cashier and is kept in a petty cash box. As small amounts of cash are used, petty cash vouchers are placed into the box stating the amounts and what they were used for. Therefore, at any time, the amount of cash left in the box plus the total amount set down on the petty cash vouchers will equal the 'imprest', the amount the float started with.

At the end of a period of time, perhaps a week, or a month, the petty cash book is brought up to date. The petty cash cashier does this by totalling the amounts taken out since the last time the book was brought up to date, and presenting the book to the cashier to claim back the amount spent. This returns the imprest to the original sum.

Petty Cash Voucher

Date 25/11/83 Folio 137

For what required	Amount £	p
Return train fare to Southampton	15	20
	15	20

Signature P. Osborn

Passed by C. Need

Dr			**Petty Cash Book**										Cr
Cash received		Date	Details	PCV	Totals		Postage		Carriage		Stationery		Sundries
£	p	1983			£	p	£	P	£	p	£	p	£	p
20	00	March 1	To Cash											
		" 3	By fares	7		74				74				
		" 5	" envelopes	8	1	00					1	00		
		" 6	" bus fares	9		50				50				
		" 8	" tea & biscuits	10	2	00							2	00
		" 11	" fares	11		74				74				
		" 12	" registered parcel	12	2	40	2	40						
		" 12	" sugar	13	1	20							1	20
		" 14	" paper clips	14	1	20					1	20		
		" 14	" window cleaner	15	3	40							3	40
		" 18	" postage stamps	16	3	00	3	00						
					16	18	5	40	1	98	2	20	6	60
			By Balance c/d		3	82								
20	00				20	00								
3	82		To Balance b/d											
16	18		To Cash											

Post Office services

There are many Post Office services that we have not mentioned and some of these are now outlined. However, for details of all these services it is suggested that the reader should look at the Post Office Guide.

In Britain we say that we have a 'two-tier' postal service. This is because we have first and second class mail. The first class service is quicker, although more expensive, than the second class service.

The Post Office has also given every address in the United Kingdom a group of letters and figures. This is the postcode, and it should always be included in an address because it helps in the mechanised sorting of mail.

Business Reply Service

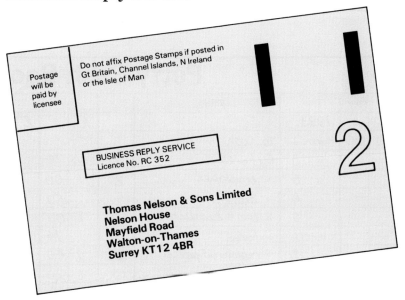

Postage
will be
paid by
licensee

Do not affix Postage Stamps if posted in
Gt Britain, Channel Islands, N Ireland
or the Isle of Man

BUSINESS REPLY SERVICE
Licence No. RC 352

Thomas Nelson & Sons Limited
Nelson House
Mayfield Road
Walton-on-Thames
Surrey KT12 4BR

This service is used mainly by businesses which wish to receive a reply from a client without putting them to the expense of paying postage. The business will enclose with their communication a specially designed, unstamped, reply card or envelope, which shows a licence number obtained from the local Head Postmaster. The cards and envelopes used for this service must be within the Post Office Preferred (POP) sizes. The client can then post back the reply card or envelope without paying any postage because it will be paid by the firm.

Freepost

Freepost is another way in which a business can receive a reply from a customer without putting them to the expense of paying postage. This is done by the firm instructing their customer to address their communication in a special way. The customer has to include the word 'Freepost' in the address.

Only the second class postal service can be used for Freepost, but it does have an advantage over the Business Reply Service in that the firm does not have to provide any postcards or envelopes. It can, for example, just publish its Freepost address in a newspaper and wait for the enquiries to come in.

The Post Office makes a yearly licence charge for both the Business Reply and Freepost services. This is in addition to the postage and the small fee which they also charge on each communication sent by these services.

Registered Post

This service should be used if any valuable items are to be sent through the post. Although a fee is charged for the use of this service, it does provide compensation if the items being sent are either lost or damaged. The fee will depend on the value of the items and the amount of compensation available.

Valuable items such as money and jewellery should only be sent through the post if registered. Indeed, if any such packets are found to be unregistered, they will be registered by the Post Office, and the fee will be charged on delivery.

Packets for registration must be handed over a post office counter. The counter clerk will then tell you how much the fee will be, and when you have paid the required amount you will be given a receipt.

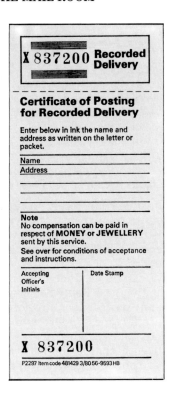

Recorded Delivery

This service is cheaper than Registered Post, but it is not suitable for sending valuables because the compensation offered is normally not high enough to make it worthwhile. It does, however, provide a record of posting and delivery, which can be very useful to a person in business. For example, it could be important to have a record of posting if a firm is sending a special document.

When a letter or parcel is being sent by Recorded Delivery it is handed over a post office counter with a special form. This form is the certificate of posting for Recorded Delivery and on it is written the name and address of the person to whom the package is being sent. The counter clerk will then initial (write their initials on) the form, date stamp it and pass it back to the sender. This now becomes proof of posting.

When the package is delivered the person who receives it will be asked to sign for it, and this is then proof of delivery.

Cash on Delivery (C.O.D.)

For a small charge the Post Office will collect a specified amount of money (not exceeding £100) from the person a parcel is being delivered to and pass it to the person who sent the parcel. This service is often used when a person is selling something but does not wish to part with the item until it has been paid for.

Poste Restante

This service allows a letter or parcel which has been marked 'Poste Restante', or 'To be called for', to be sent to the post office of a particular town or village to await collection. When the post office receives such a package they will keep it until the person to whom it is addressed collects it. It must, however, be collected within two weeks, and the person who collects it must have proof of identity.

Business people who do a great deal of travelling find this service useful, although they cannot use the same post office for longer than three months.

Datapost

The Datapost service is ideal for delivering computer data to a centre for processing. It provides a door-to-door overnight delivery service. Packages are collected from the sender at an agreed time and delivered to another address the next working morning, again at an agreed time.

Compensation Fee (CF) Parcels

Certificate of Posting

Enter below in ink the name and full address as written on the parcel and tick the appropriate box at the bottom of the form. Hand the form, together with the parcel to an officer of the Post Office. The top portion will be given back to you as a receipt. **Keep this receipt** – it should be produced if you make a claim.

Name _____

Address _____

Postcode _____

Please see notes overleaf

Accepting Officer's initials	Stamp(s) To be cancelled by accepting officer
Inland COD Form number	
Compensation Fee Paid	
Postage Paid	

Compensation up to				Date Stamp
£50	£100	£200	£300	
☐	☐	☐	☐	

Tick cover required

PP89
Revised Nov 81

Compensation Fee (CF) parcels

Compensation for loss or damage to a parcel can be claimed if a compensation fee has been paid at the time of posting. The compensation fee is payable in addition to the postage. How much the fee will be will depend on the value of the package – the greater the value, the higher the cost.

To pay a compensation fee a special certificate of posting form needs to be filled in. This form is then handed over a post office counter, together with the parcel and the appropriate fee. The counter clerk will initial and date stamp the certificate, which is then passed back to the sender who will keep it as proof of posting and payment of fee.

WHAT DO YOU KNOW?

remittance record book
Cash on Delivery
POP
Poste Restante
correspondence received book
Recorded Delivery
Post Office Guide
compensation fee
Registered
Freepost

Write out all the following sentences filling in the missing words which you can choose from the list at the side of the test.

1 A _____ can be used to record mail as it is distributed.

2 Details of all Post Office services are found in the _____.

3 When a letter enclosing a cheque is received it should be recorded in the _____.

4 The use of _____ envelopes helps the Post Office in its mechanised handling of mail.

5 _____ has an advantage over the Business Reply Service in that the sender of a letter provides their own envelope.

6 Valuable items should be sent by _____ Post.

7 With _____ the Post Office obtains a signature when it delivers a letter.

8 With the _____ service, the Post Office collects a specified amount of money from the person a parcel is being delivered to and passes it to the person who sent the parcel.

9 A package may be sent to a post office to await collection using the _____ service.

10 Compensation for loss or damage to a parcel can be claimed if a _____ has been paid.

Answer the following questions by looking back at the text in this chapter.

1 Imagine you have a new office junior working for you. Write instructions stating how to deal with incoming and outgoing mail.

2 Describe the use of the franking machine.

3 Describe how you would record the details to go in a postage book. Why do you think that a small firm is more likely to keep a postage book than a large firm?

4 What is meant by a 'two-tier' postal service?

5 Explain the difference between the Business Reply Service and Freepost.

6 Outline the difference between Registered Post and Recorded Delivery.

7 Using each as a sub-title, explain the following Post Office services:
   a Cash on Delivery
   b Poste Restante
   c Datapost
   d Compensation Fee

THINGS TO DO

1 Draw a blank petty cash book sheet similar to the one shown in this chapter. Complete the form using the following information. After totalling the different columns, bring down the balance on June 30th.

Date	PCV	Details	Amount
June 2	6	Received from cashier	50-00
June 4	7	Paid fares	3-75
June 7	8	Bought postage stamps	24-00
June 12	9	Purchased staples	1-20
June 12	10	Paid window cleaner	4-60
June 17	11	Paid fares	1-32
June 20	12	Bought tea, coffee and sugar	10-00
June 28	13	Purchased envelopes	1-30

2 Draw a blank petty cash voucher. Fill it in for the last item shown above, which was bought by yourself. The petty cashier's name was D. Batey.

3 On the reverse side of your completed petty cash sheet answer the following question:

   What is the purpose of a petty cash book?

7 TRADING DOCUMENTS

The main purpose of a business is to make a profit. Profit is the difference between the selling price of the goods sold or services provided and the cost to the company of producing those goods or services. The whole process of supplying the goods or service, from the start of the process to the end, is known as a transaction.

When transactions are taking place between businesses, documents are used to make sure that there is no confusion about what is happening. Knowledge of these documents is an important part of office work.

Trading documents move in two ways

While each firm will design its documents in a way that it feels is most suited to its business, there are certain rules which are always followed.

The letter of enquiry

TELEPHONE
SWANSEA 2934

110 TITANIC ROAD
SWANSEA SA1 5LL

Cat's Whiskers Boutique

Pricewise Clothing Co. Ltd,
89 Long Muir Avenue,
ABERDEEN,
AB1 5WT

1st June 1983

Dear Sirs,
We would be pleased to receive at your earliest convenience your catalogue and current price list of ladies clothing. Please advise current delivery period, carriage terms and cash discounts available.

Yours faithfully,
for Cat's Whiskers Boutique

Thomas Brown

T. Brown
(Head Buyer)

When a possible buyer of a product wishes to find out about the goods they are interested in buying they will send a letter of enquiry to a seller (or many sellers). This enquiry asks for such information as:

- specifications (details of the goods)
- prices
- delivery date

The enquiry may be made by letter, or it may be a printed form. If it's a printed form the required information will be filled in and it will be returned to the sender.

The quotation

PRICEWISE
Clothing Co. Ltd

89 Long Muir Avenue
ABERDEEN AB1 5WT
Telephone: Aberdeen 29287

Quotation

Cat's Whiskers Boutique,
110 Titanic Road,
SWANSEA,
SA1 5LL

4th June 1983

Dear Sirs,

We thank you for your letter of enquiry dated 1st June 1983 and we are pleased to enclose herewith our catalogue and current price list of ladies clothing.

Please note that the prices quoted are those current at the time of writing, and are only valid for a period of three months from the date of this letter, after which time a new quotation should be requested.

Current delivery is carriage paid 6 weeks from receipt of order.

Terms: 5% 7 days, 2½% 28 days, otherwise net.

Yours faithfully,

Sarah Jordan

Sarah Jordan
(Sales Manager)

When a seller receives an enquiry from a possible buyer they will want to send some form of communication showing what they can offer. They may send a specially written quotation, or an illustrated leaflet or catalogue with a price list giving details of the product – current prices, discounts and delivery terms.

Whatever method the seller uses, they will be sure to give catalogue reference numbers for each product. These numbers stop the possibility of there being any confusion where the descriptions of two products are very similar as each product has a different number.

57

The order

No.0 13448

110 TITANIC ROAD
SWANSEA SA1 5LL

TELEPHONE
SWANSEA 2934

Cat's Whiskers Boutique

ORDER

Pricewise Clothing Co. Ltd,
89 Long Muir Avenue,
ABERDEEN,
AB1 5WT

10th June 1983

QUANTITY	DESCRIPTION	PRICE
10	Shirt style blouses - Trycel White size 34 Cat. No. EA 1354	4.75
5	Super wrapover casual jackets - Red size 10 Cat. No. EM 1012	9.99
5	'French Look' hugger trousers - Blue size 12Y Cat. No. EF 4972	8.75
10	'Skinny Rib' jumpers - Black size 36/38 Cat. No. EL 5744	5.88

Deliver to Cat's Whiskers Boutique,
7 Shakespeare Crescent, SWANSEA, SA1 2SP

Thomas Brown

T. Brown
(Head Buyer)

Delivery 6 weeks from receipt of order

Please note this company will only honour official orders signed by an authorised member of this company, and will only accept goods of the standard, style and price indicated on this order.

If the possible customer finds the quotation to their liking, and decides to buy, they will send the seller an official order. This tells the seller:

- the goods required
- the agreed price
- the place of delivery
- the date of delivery.

The order will show a number in the top right-hand corner which is called the order number. This makes it easy to identify the order in the future as each order has a different number. It also makes it easy to find in a filing system.

In the example of an order opposite, it can be seen that the delivery address is different to the address from which the order has come. This can happen when a business has an administrative office at one address and a factory, warehouse or other premises somewhere else. In such a case, the invoice would be sent to the administrative address.

If an order has already been placed over the telephone a written order is usually sent as well. This is known as a confirming order, and has the word 'confirmation' typed on it in capitals. Most firms will only send goods to a customer after receiving a written order.

When the seller receives an order from a customer they will check that:

- the description matches the catalogue number quoted
- the prices quoted are correct
- the delivery requirements can be met.

The acknowledgement of order

PRICEWISE

Clothing Co. Ltd

89 Long Muir Avenue
ABERDEEN AB1 5WT
Telephone: Aberdeen 29287

11th June, 1983

We hereby acknowledge the safe receipt of your order no. 013448 and confirm that we can supply the specified goods within 6 weeks of today's date.

When the seller has checked that the information on the order is correct they will send the buyer an acknowledgement. This states that:

- they have received the order
- they are able to supply the goods
- they can meet the delivery requirements.

The acknowledgement may be in the form of a postcard, a letter, or a printed form where details of the order and delivery information have been filled in.

When the buyer receives the acknowledgement they will check it to make sure that the details are the same as on the order.

The advice note

PRICEWISE

Clothing Co. Ltd

89 Long Muir Avenue
ABERDEEN AB1 5WT
Telephone: Aberdeen 29287

Date 16th June 1983

Advice note no. AN 137892

Order no. 013448
Dated 10th June 1983
Terms: 5% 7 days
2½ % 28 days
Otherwise net

Cat's Whiskers Boutique,
110 Titanic Road,
SWANSEA,
SA1 5LL

Despatch details
1 carton
Rail 15/6/83

Quantity	Description	Price	Amount
10	Shirt style blouses - Trycel White size 34 Cat. No. EA 1354	4.75	47.50
5	Super wrapover casual jackets - Red size 10 Cat. No. EM 1012	9.99	49.95
5	'French Look' hugger trousers - Blue size 12Y Cat. No. EF 4972	8.75	43.75
10	'Skinny Rib' jumpers - Black size 36/38 Cat. No. EL 5744	5.88	58.80

Delivery to Cat's Whiskers Boutique,
7 Shakespeare Crescent, SWANSEA, SA1 2SP

An advice note is posted to the customer just before the goods are sent to them. This is to tell them to expect their arrival. If delivery is not made within a reasonable period of time (and this, of course, depends upon how far the goods have to travel) the buyer will inform the seller. The seller will then find out the reason for the delay.

This document is often a copy of the invoice. Indeed, it may carry the same number as the invoice, but with different prefix letters (the letters that go before the number). The advice note is sent to the customer's administrative office and, therefore, may show prices as well as details of the goods.

The delivery note

PRICEWISE

Clothing Co. Ltd

89 Long Muir Avenue
ABERDEEN AB1 5WT
Telephone: Aberdeen 29287

Delivery note   no. DN 137892

Date   16th June 1983

Cat's Whiskers Boutique,
110 Titanic Road,
SWANSEA,
SA1 5LL

Despatch details
1 carton
Rail 15/6/83

Order no. 013448
Dated   10th June 1983
Terms: 5% 7 days
2½ % 28 days
Otherwise net

Quantity	Description	Price	Amount
10	Shirt style blouses - Trycel White size 34 Cat. No. EA 1354		
5	Super wrapover casual jackets - Red size 10 Cat. No. EM 1012		
5	'French Look' hugger trousers - Blue size 12Y Cat. No. EF 4972		
10	'Skinny Rib' jumpers - Black size 36/38 Cat. No. EL 5744		

Delivery to Cat's Whiskers Boutique,
7 Shakespeare Crescent, SWANSEA, SA1 2SP

The delivery note is similar to the advice note and is also often a copy of the invoice, although it does not show prices. It is usually packed in with the goods, and when the buyer unpacks them they will check to see that they have received all the items stated.

When the goods are delivered by the seller's own vehicles the driver will be given a carbon copy of the delivery note, which they ask the receiver of the goods to sign. This is to confirm that the goods have been delivered.

If the goods are not delivered by the seller's own vehicles then a different document, known as a consignment note, is given to the carrier. The consignment note is similar to the delivery note, and also has to be signed by the receiver of the goods.

The invoice

PRICEWISE
Clothing Co.Ltd

89 Long Muir Avenue
ABERDEEN AB1 5WT
Telephone: Aberdeen 29287

Date   16th June 1983

Invoice no. I.137892

Order no. 013448
Dated   10th June 1983

Terms: 5% 7 days
2½% 28 days
Otherwise net

Cat's Whiskers Boutique,
110 Titanic Road,
SWANSEA,
SA1 5LL

Despatch details
1 carton
Rail 15/6/83

Quantity	Description	Price	Amount
10	Shirt style blouses - Trycel White size 34 Cat. No. EA 1354	4.75	47.50
5	Super wrapover casual jackets - Red size 10 Cat. No. EM 1012	9.99	49.95
5	'French Look' hugger trousers - Blue size 12Y Cat. No. EF 4972	8.75	43.75
10	'Skinny Rib' jumpers - Black size 36/38 Cat. No. EL 5744	5.88	58.80
			200.00
	Less 25% Trade Discount		50.00
	Amount outstanding £		150.00

Delivery to Cat's Whiskers Boutique,
7 Shakespeare Crescent, SWANSEA, SA1 2SP

E & OE

The invoice is a very important trading document. It is sent by the seller to the buyer, and states:

- the goods supplied
- how they were sent
- how much each item cost
- the total amount that the goods cost.

The most important information that the invoice gives the buyer is the amount of money that they owe the seller. Although the buyer will often pay an invoice at once, they sometimes wait until the end of the month, especially if they have bought other goods and will, therefore, receive other invoices. The buyer will then pay all the invoices together, in one payment.

Special points to look for on an invoice

- the invoice number
- the order number
- the letters E & OE
- terms – 5% 7 days, $2\frac{1}{2}$% 28 days, otherwise net.

Each invoice has a different invoice number. This makes it easy to know which invoice is being referred to at a future date.

The order number is also always stated. This is so that the buyer will know which order the invoice is dealing with.

The letters 'E & OE' are sometimes found on an invoice. They stand for the words 'errors and omissions excepted'. By this, the seller is telling the buyer that if an error (mistake) is made on the invoice they reserve the right to correct it at a later date. For example, if an invoice reads £10, but the amount owed is £100, the seller will expect the buyer to pay the correct amount when the mistake is discovered.

The wording 'Terms – 5% 7 days, $2\frac{1}{2}$% 28 days, otherwise net', refers to the discount that the buyer will receive if they pay the invoice quickly. For example, the buyer will receive 5% off the total amount of the invoice if they pay within 7 days. They will receive a discount, but only one of $2\frac{1}{2}$%, if they pay after a week, but within 28 days. However, if they take longer than 28 days to pay, then they will have to pay the full amount.

The pro-forma invoice

This looks exactly the same as the invoice, except that it has 'Pro-forma Invoice' as its title.

When a seller does not know a buyer they may not be sure that if they send the goods they will get paid for them. However, as the seller will not want to miss the opportunity of selling some of their goods, they will use a pro-forma invoice.

The pro-forma invoice is sent before the goods and charges for them in advance. When the seller receives payment they will then send the goods.

Value Added Tax (VAT)

VAT is a tax which is added to the selling price of most goods and services. The rate of this tax is decided by the Government.

When several traders are involved in the movement of goods from the producer to the consumer (the last person to buy the goods) each will charge VAT to the person to whom they sell. Each trader, however, only pays to Customs and Excise the amount of VAT they have charged their customers *less* the amount of tax paid to their suppliers.

Thus, we can see that every trader pays VAT on the difference between what they have sold the product for and what they paid for it. This difference is called the 'value added'. They, therefore, pay tax on the value they added to the product, and this is how the tax gets it name.

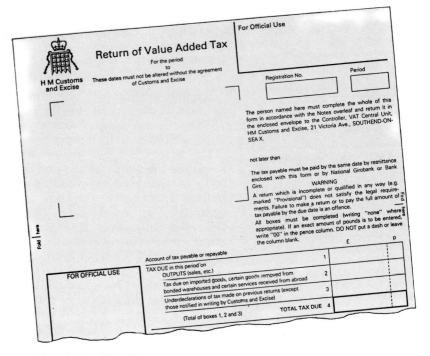

Part of Form VAT 100

Every trader must keep records of all documents relating to their business and these will tell them how much VAT they have paid and received. Either monthly, or quarterly, they enter the totals of VAT paid and received on to a form, called Form VAT 100, which they then send to the Customs and Excise. If they have received more VAT than they have paid, which is normal with most companies, they send a cheque for the difference with the form. If the opposite is true, the Customs and Excise will send them a cheque for the difference.

We said above that VAT is charged on most goods and services. Some goods and services do not have VAT charged on them because they are either zero rated or exempt.

Zero rated

Zero rated goods are those which are subject to VAT, but the rate of VAT is 0%. The trader whose goods are zero rated may reclaim all the VAT they have paid to their suppliers from the Customs and Excise.

Exempt

Exempt goods are those which are not subject to any VAT. The trader whose goods are exempt may not reclaim any VAT they have paid.

For example, a trader who sells zero rated goods may reclaim the VAT paid on their office telephone, but the trader whose goods are exempt may not.

Value on which VAT is charged

VAT is charged on the net value of the goods or service, in other words, on the value of the invoice after taking into account trade or cash discounts (even if the buyer does not take advantage of them).

Example:

	£
Gross invoice value	100-00
Less 25% trade discount	25-00
Net invoice value	75-00
Plus 15% VAT	11-25
Invoice total	86-25

Look back at the invoice on page 62. If this invoice was subject to 15% VAT the final calculations would look like this.

	5.88	58.80
		200.00
Less 25% Trade Discount		50.00
Total goods		150.00
Plus 15% VAT		22.50
Total £		172.50

Credit and debit notes

When a customer has been invoiced for goods it is sometimes found that the amount charged should be reduced. There are several reasons for this:

- A mistake has been made on the invoice and the customer has been charged too much.
- Some of the goods sent have been found to be faulty.
- Not all the goods charged for were sent.
- Packing cases which were charged for have been returned.

The document which shows the amount by which the original invoice should be reduced is called a credit note.

Remember

- Credit notes show the reason why they have been issued.
- They list the goods involved, what each costs and their total value.
- They give reference numbers of all documents involved in the transaction.
- They are usually printed in red.

PRICEWISE

Clothing Co. Ltd

89 Long Muir Avenue
ABERDEEN AB1 5WT
Telephone: Aberdeen 29287

Date   21st June 1983

Credit note   no. CN 3478

Cat's Whiskers Boutique,
110 Titanic Road,
SWANSEA,
SA1 5LL

Credit against
Order no.   013448   Dated   10th June 1983
Invoice no.   I137892   Dated   16th June 1983

Quantity		Price	Amount
	by allowance against faulty goods returned		
2	'Skinny Rib' jumpers - Black size 36 Cat. No. EL 5744	5.88	11.76
	Less 25% trade discount		2.94
	Total credit		£8.82

E & OE

The debit note has the opposite effect. It adds to the original amount owed by the customer. As in the case of a credit note, however, there are several reasons why a debit note can be issued:

- A mistake has been made on the invoice and the customer has not been charged enough.
- More goods have been sent than were charged for and the customer has agreed to keep them.

Remember

- Both credit notes and debit notes are sent by the seller.
- Both notes look very similar, but have different titles and are usually printed in different colours.
- Both notes must take into account discounts and VAT included on the original invoice.

The statement of account

PRICEWISE
Clothing Co. Ltd

89 Long Muir Avenue
ABERDEEN AB1 5WT
Telephone: Aberdeen 29287

Statement of account

Cat's Whiskers Boutique,
110 Titanic Road,
SWANSEA,
SA1 5LL,

Date 1st July 1983

Terms: 5% 7 days
2½% 21 days
Otherwise net

Date	Details	Debits	Credits	Amount
1st June	To Account Rendered May			150.30
3rd June	by Invoice I.137879	38.20		188.50
7th June	by Invoice I.137886	71.00		259.50
16th June	by Invoice I.137892	150.00		409.50
21st June	by Credit CN.3478		8.82	400.68
23rd June	by Debit DN.4166	10.00		410.68
27th June	by Cash Received		300.00	110.68

E & OE

Amount outstanding £ 110.68

When a customer buys from a particular seller on a regular basis they will probably be issued with a statement of account at the end of each month. This document will sum up all the transactions that have taken place during the last month and will also give the total amount that the customer owes.

The statement of account will show:

- Any amounts that have yet to be paid from previous statements (shown by the words 'To Account Rendered').
- Details of all invoices and debit notes that have been issued during the month. (The amounts are entered in the debit column and increase the debt owed by the customer.)
- Details of any cash received and credit notes which have been issued during the last month. (The amounts are entered in the credit column and reduce the debt owed by the customer.)
- The total amount owed by the customer at the time that the statement is issued. (This is the final figure in the amount column.)

Note: It is always best to refer to this document as the 'statement of account', rather than just the 'statement', as there is less chance of mixing it up with the bank statement.

Payment of debts

The most popular way to pay a debt is by using a cheque (see Chapter 8). There are, however, many other ways to pay a debt, including by credit transfer (see Chapter 17), or Post Office National Giro (see Chapter 10) or cash.

If cash is used to pay a debt then a receipt may be asked for to confirm that payment has been made. This is not necessary, however, when a cheque is used, or, indeed, credit transfer or Post Office National Giro. This is because these methods of payment are in themselves proof that money has been transferred.

Useful terms to know

Carriage forward	This means that the cost of delivering the goods is not included in the price and, therefore, the buyer has to pay for it.
Carriage paid	This means that the cost of delivering the goods is included in the price and is, therefore, paid by the seller.
Cash discount	This is an amount of money which is deducted from the invoice price when the debt is paid quickly.
Contract	This is a document which is usually sent by the buyer to the seller after the quotation has been accepted, and it states exactly what has been agreed.
Estimate	If a seller is unable to give a definite price for supplying a particular item or service, they will give an estimate. This is the expected, but not guaranteed, price.
Ex works	When a price is quoted 'ex works' it means that the buyer has to arrange and pay for the transporting of the goods. It is similar to 'carriage forward'.
Net	When seen on an invoice, it means that no discount has been given.
Remittance advice note	When a buyer receives a statement of account and does not want to pay the whole amount they will include this form with their payment. This form shows how much they are paying and which invoices their cheque is covering.
Tender	This is a type of quotation and is sent by several sellers who are all competing to supply the goods or services wanted by a particular buyer.
Trade discount	This is the discount given by a seller to allow a buyer in the same trade to make a profit on the resale of the goods.

WHAT DO YOU KNOW?

carriage forward

consignment note

enquiry

remittance advice note

pro-forma

estimate

order

delivery note

quotation

statement of account

Write out all the following sentences filling in the missing words which you can choose from the list at the side of the test.

1 The _____ seeks out information about products a seller has to offer.

2 The _____ is a communication which states what a seller can offer.

3 If a person finds the quotation to their liking and decides to buy, they will send the seller an official _____.

4 When the goods are delivered by the seller's own vehicles the driver will be given a copy of the _____, which they ask the receiver of the goods to sign.

5 If the goods are not delivered by the seller's own vehicles then a _____ is given to the carrier.

6 To charge for goods in advance the seller will send the buyer a _____ invoice.

7 The seller will send the buyer a _____ to sum up all the transactions that have taken place during the last month.

8 _____ means that the cost of delivering the goods is not included in the price.

9 When a seller gives an _____, it is the expected, but not guaranteed, price for a service.

10 When a buyer receives a statement of account and does not wish to pay the whole amount, they will include a _____ with their payment.

Answer the following questions by looking back at the text in this chapter.

1 Why do businesses need documents, and why is there no one style of document?

2 Explain the purpose of the letter of enquiry.

3 What is the purpose of the acknowledgement, and what information does it show?

4 Explain the purpose of the advice note, and copy the example advice note shown.

5 What are the meanings of the following when seen on an invoice?
   a Terms – 5% 7 days, $2\frac{1}{2}$% 28 days, otherwise net
   b E & OE
   c VAT

6 What is the difference between an invoice and a pro-forma invoice?

7 What is the purpose of a credit note, and why might it be sent?

8 How does the debit note differ from the credit note?

9 On a statement of account:
   a What is meant by 'To Account Rendered?'
   b Explain the debits and credits columns.

10 Explain the difference between a trade discount and a cash discount.

THINGS TO DO

You have your own trading company call Country Kitchers Ltd. which sells kitchen furniture. Produce a blank invoice similar to that shown in this chapter, but using Country Kitchens Ltd as the selling company.

Now make out the invoice with the following goods supplied to High Life Kitchens Ltd., 10 Blackgap Way, Darlington, County Durham, DL3 7UJ:

6 Sets – Circular table and 4 chairs, white
         catalogue number 340, at £84-00 per set

3 Sets – Coffee table nests
         catalogue number 215, at £50-25 per set

Prices are subject to a trade discount of 25%

15% VAT should be charged.

8 COMMERCIAL BANK ACCOUNTS

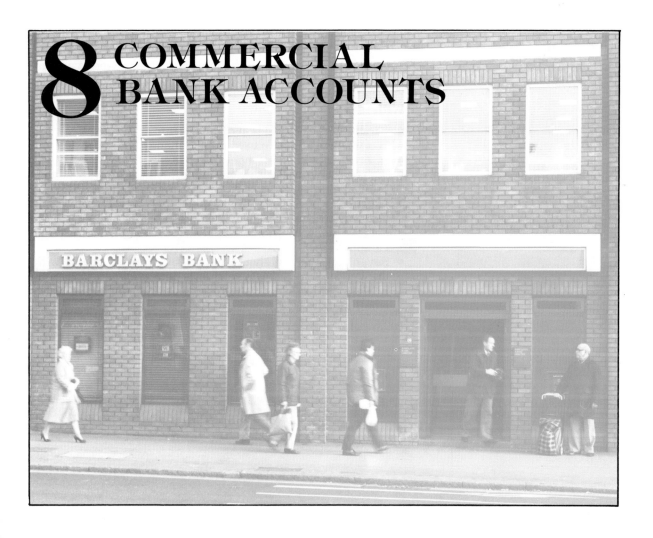

Businesses need the means to safekeep, invest and transfer money. The major institutions which provide these services are the commercial banks.

The services of the commercial banks

Commercial banks provide two main types of account for their customers – the deposit account and the current account. Money that is needed by a business to cover day-to-day running expenses will generally be kept in a current account. However, money which will not be needed immediately will probably be kept in a deposit account, where it will gain interest. Interest is an amount paid by the bank to the depositor as payment for leaving their money in the account.

The deposit account

Although interest is paid on the money kept in a deposit account the money can still be withdrawn at reasonably short notice, which can be very important to a business.

With this type of account:

- Credit slips are used to pay money into the account.
- Withdrawal slips are used to take money out of the account.
- Interest is paid on all money deposited.
- A depositor cannot draw out more money than they have in their account.
- No cheque book is given to the account holder. This means that any transfer of money to another person or business can only be done by the use of cash or a standing order (see Chapter 9).
- Seven days notice should be given before money is withdrawn. However, because this is inconvenient to account holders banks do not usually keep to this rule in the case of small amounts.

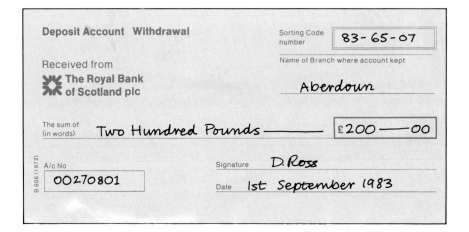

The current account

The current account is one of the most widely used accounts in business and is useful to anyone who frequently receives and pays out money.

With this type of account:

- Credit or paying-in slips are used to put money into the account.
- Cheque books are given, and cheques are used to withdraw money or transfer it to another person.
- No interest is paid. In fact, some banks will make a small charge for this service unless an agreed minimum amount, or average balance, is held in the account.

- With the bank's agreement it is possible to draw out more money than is in the account. The account is then known as overdrawn.
- No notice need be given before withdrawing money.

Paying money into a current account

Credit or paying-in slips are used to pay money into a current account. Banks do issue books with the slips already printed with the customer's name and account number, but individual credit slips are also available at the bank's counter. These slips are filled in by writing in:

- the date the deposit is being made
- the account which is to receive the money (both the account name and number is shown)
- the total amount being paid in
- the way the total has been reached (coins, notes, cheques etc.)
- the signature of the person paying in the money (this may be someone other than the account holder).

The credit slip has a counterfoil (a stub) which is filled in with the same information.

After the credit slip has been filled in, it is passed to the cashier who stamps both the slip and counterfoil. The counterfoil is then given back to the customer who keeps it as a record that the money has been paid in.

Taking money out of a current account

To take money out of a current account, or to transfer it to another person or business, a cheque is used. Banks provide two types of cheques:

- an open cheque
- a crossed cheque

A cheque is written out by filling in the following information:

- the date – which is usually the day on which the cheque is written (The cheque, however, can be post dated. This means that a date sometime in the future is given and the person it is made out to cannot present it for payment until that date arrives.)
- the name of the payee – the person the cheque is made out to
- the amount to be paid in words
- the amount to be paid in figures
- the signature of the drawer – the person from whose account the money is to be withdrawn.

The cheque should be written out clearly, leaving no spaces which could allow someone else to add more words or figures to change the amount to be paid.

The bank on which the cheque is drawn is referred to as the drawee.

Banks issue books of cheques and each cheque has an individual number. In fact, every cheque has several numbers printed on it and it is interesting to know what they all mean.

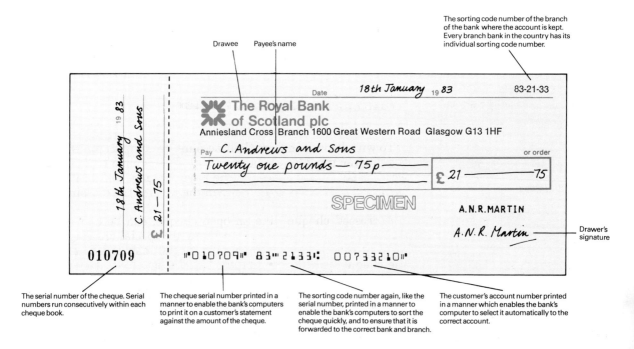

The open cheque

The open cheque is called 'open' because it is possible to get cash for it.

A person who receives an open cheque can: pay it into their own account, exchange it for cash at the drawer's bank or pass it to someone else by endorsing it (writing their signature on the back of the cheque).

While the open cheque is very flexible, it does have a drawback. This is that if it is stolen or found by someone other than the payee, *they* can also cash it at the appropriate branch of the bank. It is for this reason that banks prefer their customers to use crossed cheques.

The crossed cheque

The crossed cheque has to be paid into a bank account unless the drawer is using it to withdraw cash from their account. Open cheques can be crossed by drawing two parallel lines vertically across them, but banks do provide cheques with the crossings already printed.

To withdraw cash from their account by using a crossed cheque the drawer must 'open the crossing'. This is done by writing the word 'cash' in the space for the payee's name and writing 'pay cash' and their signature between the lines of the crossing.

A crossed cheque, like an open cheque, can be endorsed and passed on to someone else, but there are special crossings which prevent this. These crossings give special instructions as to how the cheques should be dealt with and they are written between the lines of the crossings. For example:

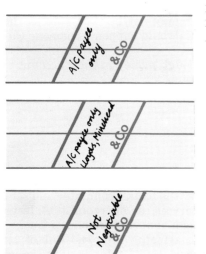

'A/c payee only' written between the crossings means that the cheque should only be paid into the account of the payee.

'A/c payee only – Lloyds, Minehead' written between the crossings means that not only should the cheque be paid into the account of the payee, but it should also be paid into a specific bank (in this case, the Minehead branch of Lloyds bank).

'Not Negotiable' written between the crossings means that the drawer does not want the cheque to be endorsed and transferred to someone else. This protects the drawer if the cheque is stolen. This is because if it is stolen and then later traced to another person's account, that person has to refund the amount shown on the cheque to the rightful owner.

Stopping a cheque

Sometimes it is necessary to stop a cheque after it has been written. This can be done by telephoning or writing to the bank, or filling in a 'stop payment' form which instructs the bank to reject the cheque when it is presented. This means that when the drawer's bank receives the cheque they will write on it 'refer to drawer' and send it back to the payee's bank which will return it to the payee. The payee must then find out from the drawer why the cheque has not been honoured (paid). This process of rejecting a cheque is sometimes called 'bouncing' a cheque.

To		Stop Payment	For Bank Use Only	Branch terminal data advice— Stop cheque entry
The Royal Bank of Scotland plc				

Branch _Anniesland Cross, Glasgow_

Date _19th January 1983_

Please stop payment of the following cheque(s)
Number(s) _010709_

Dated _18th January 1983_

Amount £ _21—75_

Payee _C. Andrews and Sons_

Drawer's Signature _A.N.R. Martin_

A/c No _00733210_

Date of Receipt   Time

F/M Code   Account Number   Amount

ADV   £

First Serial Number   Last Serial Number

* SRL   * SRL

Payee's Name

* NAR

Initials
* Delete if not applicable

F M Codes
701   Insert Stop
728   Remove Stop

BT820 (1974)

Other reasons why a cheque might bounce:

- The cheque may have been written out incorrectly.
- The signature of the drawer may not be the same as the sample held by the bank. (This would happen if someone was using a stolen cheque book.)
- The drawer may not have enough money in their account to cover the amount on the cheque.
- The cheque may be out of date. A cheque is only valid for six months after the date on the cheque.

The bank statement

A bank statement is printed out by the bank's computer and sent to each customer at regular intervals, or on request. A large business may have a bank statement sent to them once a week.

A bank statement shows all payments into and out of an account since the last statement was issued. All payments going

Statement of Account

The Royal Bank of Scotland plc

HIGH STREET ABERDOUN

Branch No.	Account No.	Page
83-6507	270 801	1

```
DONALD ROSS ESQ
28 CHARLES STREET
EASTPORT
ABERDOUN
```

Title of Account

```
DONALD ROSS
NUMBER 1 A/C
```

Abbreviations Used

ADV — Separate Advice
BGC — Bank Giro Credit
CHG — Charges
D/D — Direct Debit
DIV — Dividend received
INT — Interest
LST — List of items
S/O — Standing Order

Cheque No. or Abbreviation	Particulars	Debited £	Credited £	1983	Balance £
	BALANCE FORWARD			5 MAR	252.91
S/O	REGIONAL COUNCIL	10.30		6 MAR	242.61
D/D	GRAND INSURANCE CO	39.89		9 MAR	202.72
218755		11.53		13 MAR	
218756		5.12		13 MAR	186.07
CARD 1	CASHLINE 16 MAR	20.00		16 MAR	166.07
218758		20.00		19 MAR	
218759		1.25		19 MAR	
218761		8.34		19 MAR	
218762		20.22		19 MAR	116.26
S/O	BRITISH GAS CORP	11.00		20 MAR	105.26
S/O	MORTGAGE BLDG SOC	62.94		23 MAR	42.32
218763		20.00		23 MAR	22.32
BGC	J STEWART AND CO		306.13	30 MAR	
DIV	UNITED INVESTMENTS		14.61	30 MAR	343.06
CARD 1	CASHLINE 31 MAR	12.00		31 MAR	331.06
D/D	CAR INSURANCE LTD	30.00		2 APR	301.06
S/O	READERS BOOK CLUB	1.55		3 APR	299.51

Lists	Debit Vouchers	Total Debited £	Total Credited £	1983	Balance £
	7	274.14	320.74	3 APR	299.51

DR: Account Overdrawn

out of an account are put in the payments or debits column, and all payments going into an account are shown in the receipts or credits column. The balance is the amount of money in an account and a new balance is shown every time a payment or receipt is made.

Clearing cheques

The process of passing a cheque through the banking system so that the payee's account receives the money (is credited) and the drawer's account has the money taken out (is debited), is known as the clearing system.

If both the payee and the drawer use the same branch of a bank then the process is simple. The bank will just transfer on paper the value of the cheque from the drawer's account to the payee's account.

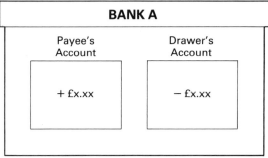

Branch 1

If the payee uses the same bank, but a different branch from the drawer, then the cheque will be sent to the head office of the bank and on to the branch of the drawer. The value of the cheque will then be sent in return.

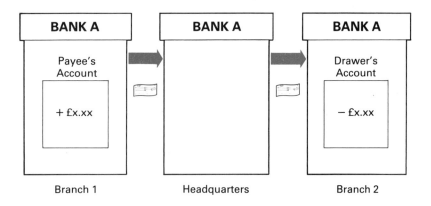

However, if the payee and drawer use different banks then the process is more complicated. To follow this process look at the diagram opposite. The payee uses Branch 1 of Bank A, and the drawer uses Branch 3 of Bank B.

Note: At the Clearing House a record is kept of the value of the piles of cheques changing hands. The difference between the value of the cheques received and handed over shows how much each of the banks owes the others. This information is used daily to credit (add to) or debit (deduct from) the balances of the clearing banks which are kept at the Bank of England. A clearing bank is a bank whose cheques are sorted through the London Bankers' Clearing House.

The cheque is presented at the payee's local branch (Branch 1) and the cheque, together with all the other cheques apart from those belonging to people with accounts at that branch, are sent to the head office of Bank A.

At the head office the cheques are sorted into piles of each of the other major banks and a representative from Bank A then takes these cheques to the Clearing House. (Bank A's **own** cheques are sent on to its various branches.)

At the Clearing House the representative from Bank A will meet the representatives from the other banks and they will exchange their cheques so that they all receive the cheques belonging to their bank.

The representatives will then return to their head offices with their cheques and therefore the representative from Bank B will return to Bank B's head office. At the head office of Bank B the cheques will be sorted into piles of each of the different branches and therefore the cheque in question will be sent to Branch 3.

At Branch 3 the drawer's account will be debited to the amount written on the cheque.

WHAT DO YOU KNOW?

clearing
interest
credit slips
crossed
stop payment
credits
bouncing
current
balance
'account payee'

Write out all the following sentences filling in the missing words which you can choose from the list at the side of the test.

1 _____ is the payment given to a depositor for leaving their money in a deposit account.

2 _____ are used to put money into either a deposit account or a current account.

3 No interest is paid on the money kept in a _____ account.

4 Banks provide two types of cheques: an open cheque and a _____ cheque.

5 A cheque should only be paid into the payee's account when it has been crossed _____.

6 A _____ form instructs the bank to reject the cheque when it is presented.

7 The process of rejecting a cheque is sometimes called _____ a cheque.

8 All payments going into an account are shown in the receipts or _____ column of a bank statement.

9 The _____ is the amount of money in an account.

10 A _____ bank is a bank whose cheques are sorted through the London Banker's Clearing House.

Answer the following questions by looking back at the text in this chapter.

1 How do you put money into and take money out of a deposit account? How does this account differ from the current account?

2 Explain the meaning of the word 'interest' in relation to the deposit account.

3 Explain the terms: payee, drawer and drawee.

4 With the aid of diagrams, explain the difference between open and crossed cheques.

5 Under what circumstances might one open the crossing of a cheque, and how might one do so?

6 Draw and explain the three special cheque crossings shown in this chapter.

7 Under what circumstances might a cheque not be passed for payment?

8 Explain the purpose of the payments, receipts and balance columns of the bank statement.

9 Explain the process of clearing a cheque when the payee and the drawer use the same bank, but different branches.

10 Explain the process of clearing a cheque when the payee and drawer use different banks.

THINGS TO DO

1 Obtain, or draw, a paying-in slip for a current account at a bank. Complete it using the following information.
   Cash: £80-00 in £5 notes; £48-00 in £1 coins; £18-00 in 50p pieces; £36-00 in silver; 90p in copper.
   Cheques: £265-30; £172-80; £75-00.
   Postal order: £4-00.

2 Draw a cheque and fill it in to pay a friend £65-29. Cross the cheque in a way that will make sure that only your friend can pay it into their account.

3 Draw up a simple page of analysis columns (balance, date, credited, debited etc.) similar to the example of a statement of account shown on page 77.

Carry forward the balance shown on that statement and then record the following transactions that Donald Ross has put into effect, and balance the account for each transaction.

5 APR	Cashline	20.00 −
7 APR	Cheque 218764 (Scott)	160.30 −
10 APR	BGC J. Greaves	98.50 +
15 APR	Cheque 218765 (Kent)	96.30 −
23 APR	Mortgage Bldg Soc	62.94 −
30 APR	BGC J. Stewart and Co	328.88 +

9 OTHER SERVICES OF THE COMMERCIAL BANKS

As well as offering the means to invest and transfer money while keeping it safe, the commercial banks also provide a variety of other services which are very useful to both businesses and private individuals.

Standing orders

If a company buys a piece of equipment which has to be paid for by monthly payments they normally arrange to pay these by standing order. To do this the firm will fill out a standing order form which instructs their bank to make regular payments to a specific person, or company, for a particular period of time, or until further notice in writing.

   This service is offered to all bank customers and saves anyone who uses it the task of remembering to make the regular payments themselves.

To **The Royal Bank of Scotland plc**

Standing Order

Please make the payments detailed below and debit my/our account

Name of A/c to be debited	DONALD ROSS
Reference No to be quoted (if any)	—
Name of Payee	MORTGAGE BUILDING SOCIETY
Address of Payee	CHARLES STREET
	GLASGOW
Bank & Branch to which payment is to be made	THE ROYAL BANK OF SCOTLAND
	ANNIESLAND CROSS BRANCH
	GLASGOW
Amount (in words)	SIXTY-TWO POUNDS
	SIXTY-TWO POUNDS, NINETY-FOUR PENCE
Date of payments	23RD OF EACH MONTH
Date of first payment	23RD MARCH 1983
Special instructions (if any)	—

A/c No 00270801

Date 7th March 1983

A/c No 00689254

Code No 83-21-33

£ 62 — 94

* Payments are to continue until ___
(date of last payment inclusive)
* Payments are to continue until you receive further notice in writing

Signature D. Ross

B1367 (1971)

*Delete as necessary

Direct debit

This is a variation of the standing order system. Instead of instructing the bank to make regular payments on their behalf, the customer fills in a form which allows the person, or firm, to whom they owe money, to withdraw regular amounts from their account. The amount to be withdrawn may vary from time to time.

Bank giro credit

The bank giro credit system can be used by bank customers and non-customers. The system can be used for settling bills or for paying into a bank account when away from home. There are two basic ways to use the system:

1 Credit transfer – single transfer method

A bank giro credit form, similar to the following example, is filled out with the:

- date
- details of account to be credited
- amount to be transferred
- signature.

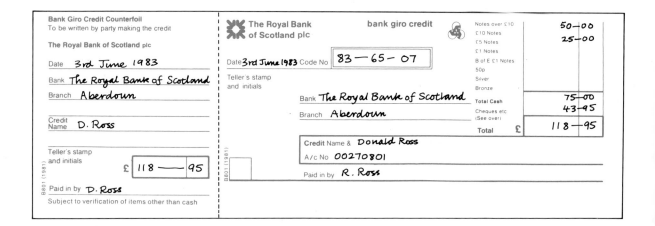

The money to be transferred can be paid into the bank by cash, cheque or postal order. Most of the State-owned domestic suppliers, such as gas, electricity and water boards help their customers to use this system by printing bank giro credit forms at the bottom of their bills.

2 Credit transfer – multiple transfer method

By using this method a customer only needs to write one cheque to pay several bills. They do this by filling out a bank giro credit transfer schedule, which lists all amounts and accounts to be credited, and writing a cheque to cover the total amount on the schedule.

For example: instead of writing out a cheque for each employee when it's time to pay the wages, a business will provide its bank with a schedule, listing all the amounts to be paid and details of the accounts of its employees, and a cheque to cover the total amount. The bank will then transfer the various amounts to the correct accounts and the company merely advises its employees how much they have been paid.

Sorting Code No	For the Account of			Amount
01-72-09	J Davidson	Lloyds	Hightown	230.86
07-47-37	L McDonald	Barclays	Hometown	350.94
15-88-41	A Grant	Nat West	Lowtown	528.24
07-33-46	J Brown	Barclays	Hightown	333.09
11-74-66	R Godfrey	Midland	Hometown	428.15
11-37-06	S Stone	Midland	Lowtown	331.13
15-32-70	P Eustace	Nat West	Hometown	339.00
01-22-71	D Batey	Lloyds	Hightown	332.47
01-18-83	J O'Bryan	Lloyds	Downtown	423.55
24-62-11	G Hamilton	R B Scotland	Lowtown	280.30
15-44-17	B McPherson	Nat West	Anytown	261.50
11-32-33	K Sampson	Midland	Hometown	311.00
24-36-26	D James	R B Scotland	Anytown	530.96
07-66-16	J Ward	Barclays	Hightown	720.36

To The Royal Bank of Scotland plc, St Andrew Square Office, 36 St Andrew Square, Edinburgh EH2 2YB

Sheet No 1. Date 20th November 1983. Please distribute the bank giro credit transfers attached as arranged by us with the recipients, Our cheque for:- £ 5401.55 is enclosed.

for Sweyne Trading PLC. Authorised Signature(s) John Ward, Director. Original

Bank giro credit transfers totalling £5401.55 will be distributed in accordance with the details thereon

Branch Stamp and initials. Date. B 1371

A multiple transfer schedule

85

Bank cards

Cheque card

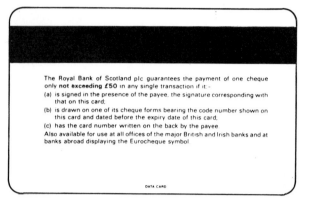

A cheque card is used to:

- Guarantee payment of a cheque up to the amount shown on the card.
- Present with a cheque when a person wants to withdraw cash from their account at a branch or bank other than their own. This allows a person to obtain cash up to the amount shown on the card.

Credit card

A person who has one of these cards can use it to buy goods and services from a trader who belongs to the scheme.

This means that no cash or cheques are used. The cardholder just presents the card and signs a voucher. The trader claims the money from the issuer of the card and has the amount credited to his account.

Once a month the cardholder is sent a statement of account from the issuer of the card. The cardholder can then settle the account all at once, or just pay a part of it. The outstanding amount will be carried over to the next month's statement and interest will be charged on it.

Credit cards are usually issued by special credit card companies, such as Access, American Express or Diners Club, although some banks, such as Barclays, use one card as a combined credit and cheque card.

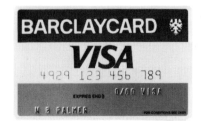

Cash dispenser card

A cash dispenser is a machine set in the outside wall of some banks. The customer is given a card which they put into the machine. They then tap out on a keyboard a personal number, known only to themselves and the bank's computer, and the amount of cash required. The machine will then release the money and the computer will automatically debit the cardholder's account. The dispenser will only pay out in fixed amounts and only up to the maximum allowed.

The machine is available for use 24 hours a day, weekends and holidays included.

Bank overdrafts and loans

As stated in the last chapter, it is possible, with permission from the bank, for a person to write out cheques for more money than they have in their current account, up to an agreed amount. When this happens the account is known as being overdrawn or 'in the red'. The actual amount that the account is overdrawn by is known as the overdraft.

Irrespective of how much money the bank gives them permission to overdraw their account by, the customer is only charged interest on the actual amount overdrawn. The interest due is calculated daily. Any deposits, therefore, made to the account while it is overdrawn will reduce the overdraft, while any cheques paid out will increase it.

If a person has a bank loan, however, the bank transfers the total value of the loan to their account, and, therefore, even if the customer does not draw all the money out immediately, they will still be required to pay interest on the whole amount.

The customer repays the loan, including interest, by making regular payments of a set amount which has been agreed with the bank.

Additional services

Commercial banks offer a number of other services, such as:

- Providing a night safe, so that traders can bank their day's takings after the bank has shut.
- The safe keeping of valuable documents.
- Supplying foreign currency and traveller's cheques.
- Investment advice.
- Advising on taxation and trusts.

A night safe

Most banks have a special counter for supplying foreign currency and traveller's cheques

WHAT DO YOU KNOW?

bank giro credit
cheque card
bank loan
night safes
standing order
overdraft
wages
cash dispenser
credit card
multiple transfer

Write out all the following sentences filling in the missing words which you can choose from the list at the side of the test.

1 A _____ instructs your bank to make regular payments on your behalf.

2 The _____ system can be used by bank customers and non-customers.

3 Employees may be paid their _____ by credit transfer.

4 By using the _____ method of credit transfer a customer need only write one cheque to pay several bills.

5 Having used a _____ it is not possible to stop payment of the cheque.

6 The _____ allows the holder to buy goods or services without using cash or cheques.

7 A _____ provides a 24 hour banking service.

8 Someone with an _____ is sometimes said to be 'in the red'.

9 A _____ is repaid by regular payments.

10 Commercial banks provide _____ so that traders can deposit their day's takings after the banks have shut.

Answer the following questions by looking back at the text in this chapter.

1 Describe the standing order service, giving at least two examples of when it might be used by:
   a an individual
   b a business

2 How does the direct debit differ from the standing order service?

3 Outline the bank giro system, taking care to point out the differences between the single and multiple transfer services.

4 What is the purpose of a cheque card?

5 What is the purpose of the credit card and how might it be used to reduce the number of entries on a customer's bank account?

6 'The cash dispenser card gives 24 hour banking.' Explain this statement.

7 In what way does a bank overdraft differ from a bank loan?

THINGS TO DO

1 You have arranged to purchase a typewriter which you will pay for by twelve monthly payments of £10-00, starting on the fifth day of next month. You intend to pay these instalments by means of a standing order taken out against your current account, number 753149.
   a Draw a blank standing order form.
   b Complete the form instructing the bank to make the payments on your behalf. Make the payments to a firm whose name you should find from a newspaper advertisement.

2 Your trading company, Country Kitchens Ltd, wishes to pay its employees' monthly salaries by credit transfer. Draw a blank credit transfer schedule and complete it for the following payments. Use today's date and Sheet no. 64. Do not forget to sign it.

Bank code	Bank and branch	Payee's name	Amount
11-813	Midland, Basildon	S. Trigg	£218-64
120-14	Barclays, Loughton	P. Eustace	£183-12
120-14	Barclays, Grays	D. Batey	£169-15
53-710	Lloyds, Rayleigh	L. Perry	£258-04

3 Assuming the previous balance in your firm's bank account was £1,860-50, how much now remains in the account?

10 THE POST OFFICE BANKING SYSTEM

The Post Office offers a number of services which are useful for both saving and transferring money. Some of these services are used directly by businesses and others are used by their customers when paying for their goods or services.

Postal orders

These are a simple way of transferring money. They are issued by the Post Office in varying amounts of 5p up to a maximum of £10. If a person wants to transfer more than £10, then they have to buy however many postal orders are needed to make up the required amount.

To cover the cost of providing this service the Post Office makes a small charge on every postal order. This small charge is called poundage.

Reproduced by permission of the Post Office

To send a postal order a person must fill in:

- the payee's name in ink
- the name of the post office of payment.

The value of a postal order may be increased up to 4p by sticking one or two stamps in the place provided.

A postal order has a counterfoil which is filled in and kept as proof of purchase. It is also used to reclaim the money if the postal order is lost. The life of a postal order is six months. The postal order, like a cheque, can be crossed, which means that it cannot be cashed at a post office, but has to be paid into a bank account.

National Girobank

The Post Office offers this banking service which provides a means of safekeeping, transferring and investing money.

Although National Girobank does not offer such a wide range of services as the commercial banks, it does have an advantage in that all accounts are held at one centre – at the Girobank head office at Bootle, Merseyside. This means that its clearing system for cheques is much simpler and less expensive than the commercial banks' clearing system (see Chapter 8).

Any person or business can open an account with National Girobank by depositing £10, or more, at any post office. Although all accounts are held at Bootle, an account holder can deposit money at any post office and withdraw money (up to £50) from their account, on every other business day, from either of two post offices which they have already named. Before larger amounts can be withdrawn, or before money can be withdrawn from a post office other than those named, cheques have to be first sent to Bootle for clearance.

National Girobank provides its account holders with:

Cheque books These allow cash to be withdrawn from accounts, and money to be transferred to other people.

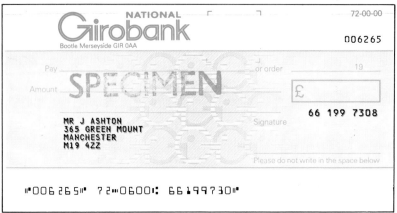

A Girobank cheque

Reproduced by permission of the Post Office

A Guarantee Card This is for customers aged 18 or over, to allow them to withdraw up to £50 from any post office.

Reproduced by permission of the Post Office

Transfers and standing orders These are convenient ways to pay other Girobank customers. Many household bills, such as gas, electricity, telephone and water, already have a Girobank transfer form attached.

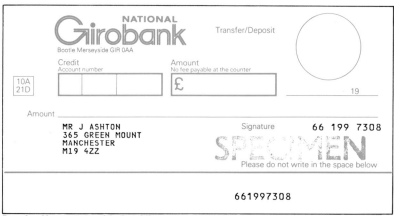

Reproduced by permission of the Post Office

Envelopes These (with free first-class postage) are for sending transfers and cheques to National Girobank.

Deposit accounts These give a good rate of interest on savings, plus bonus interest paid on the minimum balance held in each six monthly period.

Budget accounts These help spread the cost of paying bills evenly throughout the year.

Bridging loans These are to help finance the cost of moving house.

Foreign currency and Thomas Cook travellers' cheques These can be ordered at most post offices and will then be sent by registered post to the customer's address.

Giro statements These show details of payments, receipts and charges, and also the current balances, of individual accounts.

No charges are made on ordinary current account banking services as long as the account remains in credit.

STATEMENT OF ACCOUNT 1FEB83

Number 66 199 7308

NATIONAL Giirobank
Bootle Merseyside GIR 0AA

◀G70

Serial 179

VAT registration number 243 1700 02

Transactions

Summary

previous balance	22JAN83	£102.72
total debits		81.71
total credits		114.41
current balance	1FEB83	£135.42

DEBITS £

23JAN	T	6123208	NORWEB	24.86
24JAN	T	6132108	NWGB	16.24
26JAN	S	6103121	GIRO LNS	25.05
28JAN	C	001412		7.00
30JAN	C	001410		8.56
1FEB		CREDITS		
	T	0618704015		19.25
	D	SELF		20.00
	T	WAGES		75.16

MR J ASHTON
365 GREEN MOUNT
MANCHESTER
M19 4ZZ

C Cheque
D Deposit
OD Overdrawn

T Transfer
TC Transcash
DD Direct Debit

S Standing Order
A Automatic
debit transfer

Enquiries: Please contact your Regional Office, where this has been notified to you, otherwise, National Girobank, Bootle, Merseyside, GIR 0AA, (telephone 051-928 8112).

Produced by permission of the Post Office

A Girobank statement

National Girobank services for non-account holders

Reproduced by permission of the Post Office

Non-customers can use Girobank to pay money to people and organisations who do hold National Girobank accounts. This is particularly useful because it avoids the cost of envelopes and postage. Cash payments can be made at a post office by filling in a Transcash form, although many organisations already include inpayment forms on their bills.

To take up this service:

- Inpayment must be made using Girobank Transcash forms, or a form provided by the account holder.
- A small nominal charge is payable by a non-customer for each inpayment, except where the account holder has provided an inpayment form.
- Payment must be made in cash. Cheques are not accepted.

As well as its money transfer services the Post Office also provides several savings and investment schemes.

National Savings Bank accounts

There are two types of Post Office Savings Bank accounts, both of which pay interest to savers:

- ordinary accounts
- investment accounts, which offer a higher rate of interest.

Ordinary accounts

This type of account can be opened by a deposit of 25p or more at any one of over 20,000 savings bank post offices in the United Kingdom.

The National Savings Bank issues depositors with a bank book in which all transactions are recorded. In other words, all deposits and withdrawals are recorded in the book, including any interest gained by leaving money in the account.

There are a variety of ordinary accounts available:

Individual accounts These are available to anyone who is seven years of age or over. An individual may hold more than one account.

Children's accounts These may be opened by an adult on behalf of a child below seven years of age.

Joint accounts These are for two or more persons. However, all parties to the account must sign any withdrawal form.

Trust accounts These may be opened by one or more people on behalf of another person. If the account is for a child they are not allowed to withdraw any money while they are under seven years of age.

Society accounts These are available for clubs and organisations.

Paying money into an ordinary account

- cash
- cheque, as long as the cheque has not been crossed to a particular bank, other than the Bank of England
- stamp savings books
- gift tokens
- transfer from a National Girobank account.

Deposits are entered immediately in the bank book by the post office cashier.

Taking money out of an ordinary account

Withdrawals of up to £100 on demand can be made by completing a withdrawal slip and presenting it at a post office.

Withdrawals can also be made by:

- warrant, payable at a specified post office
- crossed warrant, payable through a bank

Interest is paid on every complete pound and is added to the account at the close of each year.

NATIONAL SAVINGS BANK   **6**

APPLICATION FOR A WITHDRAWAL FROM AN **ORDINARY ACCOUNT**

1 Enter **IN BLOCK LETTERS** the Account Particulars exactly as printed in the Bank Book.

Office, code words, or letters (if any)

No.

2 I, the depositor in the account, wish to withdraw:–

POUNDS   PENCE

£

If account is to be closed, state balance in book and add here the words "to close account" ....

Complete

A

In Cash, on production of the bank book,

at... Post Office

3 or

B

By Crossed Warrant, payable through a Bank, or the National Giro to the account of:–

BLOCK LETTERS

The bank book must be sent with this application for a **CROSSED WARRANT.** Crossed warrants are not issued for amounts under **£1.**

(If payment is to be made direct to the Giro Centre, enter below the number of the Giro account to be credited and enclose a completed Giro deposit form for that account.)

4 Signature.. Date........................197......

5 Name and Address (including postcode) IN BLOCK LETTERS for reply.

M...

....

....

See over

HEAD OFFICE USE ONLY

	LAST XN		B. BAL			PEN XN	
Code		£	£		Code	£	

SUM AUTHORISED			Mult. Wts.	New Book	Overprint No./Office Code			
	POUNDS	PENCE						
....			Date	Entd.	Fms.	Advd.	Exd
..........................pounds							
....							

Investment accounts

This type of account can be opened with a deposit of £1 or more at any savings bank post office. As with the ordinary account, the investment account holder is issued with a bank book in which all transactions are recorded.

Deposits to this account may be made in the same way as those for ordinary accounts, but in addition, they may also be made by transferring money from an ordinary account.

All withdrawals need one month's notice in writing, beginning with the day on which the application is received at the head office. In other words, payments on demand are not allowed. The bank book is examined each time a withdrawal application is made.

As with the ordinary account, interest is paid on every complete pound, and the interest is added to the account at the end of each year. The rate of interest depends on how much can be earned when the money is invested in Government and other securities. However, the interest received is higher than that paid on ordinary accounts, and the current rate can be obtained from any post office.

Save As You Earn (SAYE)

The National Savings Bank SAYE service offers a form of saving linked to the Retail Prices Index and aims to offset the effect of price rises (inflation) on savings.

In this scheme the saver agrees to make monthly payments of a fixed amount, of between £4 and £20, over a period of five years. At the end of the five year contract period, the saver can take repayment of their investment. At this time each payment is revalued in line with changes in the General Index of Retail Prices between the time of investment and the month of repayment.

Alternatively, the saver can leave their savings invested for a further two years without making any further payments. The value of the savings are again changed to be in line with the Prices Index at the time of repayment, and at the same time, a bonus, equal to the monthly payments, is also paid.

SAYE contracts can be held by anyone over the age of 16 years. Payments can be made through:

- a post office, where monthly payments are made by cash or by standing order on a National Girobank account
- a bank, using the standing order service
- an employer, who takes part in the SAYE service and will deduct monthly payments from the employee's salary.

WHAT DO YOU KNOW?

transfer form
joint accounts
investment accounts
poundage
SAYE
ordinary account
counterfoil
non-customers
bank books
National Girobank

Write out all the following sentences filling in the missing words which you can choose from the list at the side of the test.

1 The charge for purchasing a postal order is called _____.

2 A postal order has a _____ which is filled in and kept as proof of purchase.

3 With _____ all accounts are held at one centre.

4 National Girobank services can be used by customers and _____.

5 Many household bills have a Girobank _____ attached.

6 National Girobank _____ are for two or more persons.

7 The National Savings Bank issues depositors with _____.

8 With a National Savings Bank _____ withdrawals of up to £50 on demand can be made.

9 Withdrawals from National Savings Bank _____ need one month's notice in writing.

10 The _____ service is a form of saving which is linked to the Retail Prices Index to offset the effect of inflation.

Answer the following questions by looking back at the text in this chapter.

1 In relation to postal orders, explain each of the following:
   a poundage
   b payee
   c life of a postal order

2 How might the value of a postal order be increased, and how might it be made 'safe'?

3 What is the main advantage that the National Girobank has over the commercial banks' cheque system?

4 Describe the services Girobank provides for its account holders.

5 What service does Girobank offer non-customers and what conditions apply to this service?

6 Explain the difference between the National Savings Bank ordinary account and the National Savings Bank investment account.

7 Describe the SAYE service and explain the purpose of the two alternative contract periods.

THINGS TO DO

1 Draw an example of a Girobank transfer/deposit form (see page 92).
Fill in this form using the following information:
your giro account number is 48 509 2744 and you want to pay in £20-00. Use today's date.

2 Visit your local post office and find out:
   a The current rate of interest on National Savings ordinary accounts and National Savings investment accounts.
   b The current maximum balance an account holder is allowed to hold in each of these accounts.

11 METHODS OF FILING

Filing is the storing of correspondence, records or documents in folders, pockets or binders on shelves or in cabinets.

Why do we file?

We file to keep:

- papers tidy
- papers safe
- papers where they can be found easily and quickly when needed.

For these reasons a good filing system must be:

- simple and easy to use
- secure, to protect confidential information
- suitable for the type of material it must contain
- placed in a good position, so that it is within easy reach of those who will need to use it
- consistent, to avoid confusion.

Where is filing done?

Each department may do its own filing or it may be done in a special centralised filing department.

Departmental filing

Departmental filing means that each department of the firm will carry out its own filing.

Advantages

- Papers can be found quickly. It takes time for a file to be obtained from a centralised filing department, especially if it is at the other end of the building, or in a different building.
- Files can easily be referred to while someone is on the telephone.
- Those concerned with the files are more likely to know about their contents, as they will probably be dealing with the matters referred to on file.
- Filing is often done when other work is slack. This means that the staff will be kept busy when there is little else to do.

Centralised filing

Centralised filing means that a single department is responsible for the filing of all the firm's documents. The various departments of the firm will bring their filing to a central room and hand it to the staff of the centralised filing department who will then deal with it. When a department wishes to obtain a document from the files, someone will go to one of the filing clerks. The clerk will then find the document and pass it over.

Centralised filing departments are usually found in firms where different departments need the same files.

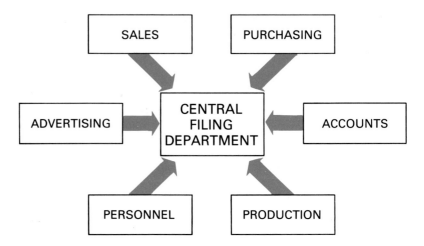

With centralised filing documents from all departments are sent to a central room for filing

Advantages

- It reduces wastage of filing space.
- The filing staff tend to be more efficient at filing than those who file only occasionally.
- It is easy to keep a check on the files and follow up any missing papers.
- It is clear who is responsible for filing.
- All the records are kept in one place and relevant information from all departments will be filed together.

If an individual, or department, needs a file or document, the member(s) of staff responsible for the files will want to have a record of who has taken it. This means that if the papers are not returned, they can chase up the borrower. A record of a borrower of a file or a document can be kept by using either:

- a charging-out form
- an out guide.

The charging-out system

The charging-out system requires the borrower of papers to fill in a charging-out form. This form shows the following information:

- title of the papers borrowed
- name of the person and/or the department who is borrowing it
- date
- signature of the borrower
- a follow-up date to check for the return of the papers.

The out guide

	OUT		
Date	File	Taken by	Returned
5th May	H. Haynes and Co.	M. Roberts (Accounts)	8th May J.W.
15th June	R. Jones and Partners	A. Smith (Sales)	16th June J.W.
18th June	Brown Bros.	R. Toms (Sales)	

An out guide can be used many times. Note that the filing clerk has initialled the card when the file has been returned.

When papers, or a complete file, are removed from the storage space, it is useful to put an out guide in their place. This card is often coloured, which draws attention to the fact that something is missing from the file, and it will have an index tab, which sticks up with the word 'out' printed in large letters. The card will usually be filled in with details of the missing document and the name of the person who has borrowed it, although sometimes it will have a pocket into which is put a charging-out form.

Cross referencing

CROSS-REFERENCE CARD	
For	Look under
Miss Dorothy Stephenson	Mrs D. Carter

Why do you think it has been necessary to raise this cross-reference card?

There may be times when the papers in one file also refer to those in another. Alternatively, a complete file may have been taken from one part of the filing system to another, perhaps because of a change in name. In such a case, a cross-reference card will be completed and put into the file or storage space that is less likely to be used.

When is filing done?

- Within a centralised filing department filing is carried out all the time.
- Within departments filing is usually done when other work is slack.

However, papers should be filed as soon as possible so that they can be found easily if needed. While documents are waiting to be filed they should be placed in a tray or basket marked 'filing'.

How long are papers kept on file?

The length of time (document retention period) that a firm will keep papers will depend on company policy. This will be decided to a certain extent by the amount of storage space they have available. Firms are obliged by law, however, to keep some records for a number of years.

Some firms will store the files that are not used very often in basement archives (special places where records are kept) until they can be destroyed. Some firms destroy their old files by burning them in an incinerator. Other firms feed the papers through a shredding machine. This machine will cut up the papers to make them impossible to read. After the papers have been shredded they will either be put out as rubbish or given to a waste paper merchant.

A shredding machine being used to destroy confidential documents

Methods of classification

When letters and documents do not have their own subject folders they are kept in a miscellaneous folder. In some departments there will be just one miscellaneous folder with the various correspondence filed alphabetically. In other departments there will be a separate miscellaneous folder for each letter of the alphabet.

However, when the correspondence with a particular firm, or on a particular subject, is large enough, or looks as if it will continue for some time, it is placed in its own file folder. This folder will then be given a title and filed under one of the filing systems.

There are several different methods of filing to choose from, and which one is used, will depend on the type of correspondence being filed.

The five most popular methods of filing are:

- alphabetical – in alphabetical order of name
- numerical – in number order
- geographical – by area, town or country
- subject – by the subject of the papers
- chronological – in date order

Some departments will use a combination of these systems.

The alphabetical method

The most popular method of filing in business is the alphabetical method and it is the basis of most of the other systems. It is, therefore, most important to understand this system.

Alphabetical filing rules

Personal names

As far as filing is concerned, the surname is considered first. File according to the first letter of the surname:

Adams, A.
Baker, D.W.
Clark, B.E.
Dunn, R.

If all the first letters of the surname are the same, then sort out the order on the second letters. If the second letters are the same, then use the third letters, and so on:

Adams, A.
Angus, R.T.
Atman, B.E.
Atwood, V.K.

If all the letters in the surname are the same, then file according to initials:

Adams, A.A.
Adams, A.C.
Adams, J.M.

If all the letters in the surname are the same, remember, 'nothing before something' and 'short comes before long'. Always put a surname alone, before a surname with initials, and put a surname with initials, before a surname with a first name:

Barron,
Barron, H.
Barron, H.R.
Barron, David
Barron, James, P.
Barron, Hugh, Charles

Ignore titles:

Davis, A.B.
Davis, Sir. F.T.
Davis, Dr. M.B.
Davis, Capt. S.N.

When a name includes a hyphen, ignore the hyphen and file as one continuous word, starting from the *first* part of the hyphenated name:

Sims, F.
Sims-Brown, H.
Sims-Johnson, L.
Simson, A.
Sims-Smith, R.

Prefixes to surnames

Prefixes such as M', Mc and Mac are all considered as if spelt 'Mac', and they are filed alphabetically according to the letters after the prefix:

MacAndrew, N.R.
McAndrew, Peter
MacAngus, W.
McArthur, R.
MacAulay, D.

Prefixes such as De, O', Van, are considered as part of the surname they prefix:

De Hain, T.
De Havilland, C.
O'Casey, P.
O'Keefe, L.
Van Dam, E.
Van Der Beer, A.

The prefix St. should be considered as 'Saint':

St. Andrew's Hospital
Saint Andrew's School
Saint Clair's College
St. Pancras Station

Company names

If the name of a company includes a personal name, consider the surname first:

John Jones Estates
Adrian Kate Laundry
Arthur J. Watson & Co.

Where business names do not include the full personal name, they are filed in the order in which they are written:

Davidson Duplicating Services
Davidson Enterprises
Edwards Cleaning Company
Edwards Hardware

If a name of a company includes initials as part of its name then file it, according to the initials, before a company without initials:

A.B.C. Taxis
A.R.P. Builders
Abbey National
Ace Employment Agency

Numbers are treated as if printed in full:

5 Star Laundry
4 Star Cafe
4 Ways Printers
20th Century Fox

Ignore 'The' and all conjunctive (joining) words, such as, of, on, for, and:

Baker of Bankside
Baker and Company
The British Bridge Company
Buffers for Books

Municipal names (names which refers to towns, cities or their local governments), require the place name to be considered first:

Hawley, Parish of
Rochford, District Council of
Southend, Corporation of

Ignore 'Co.' and 'Ltd':

Tapes & Boxes Ltd
Tapes Carpet Co. Ltd
Tapes Cranes & Co.
Tenby Trading Co. Ltd.

In the case of official or descriptive names, file in accordance with the most important words in the title. This will often mean that the name is reversed:

Harlow, Public Library of
Health and Social Security, Department of
Historical Society, Canvey Island
Historical Studies, School of

Guides to help the filing clerk

To help the filing clerk to find the exact file quickly the following guides are used. (Although they refer to the alphabetical filing method they can be used with any filing system.)

Drawer guides These are placed on the front of each drawer of the cabinet. For example, A-D, E-K, L-R, S-Z.

Primary guides These have index tabs which stick up. They are put on the left-hand side of file sections. For example, A, B, C.

Secondary guides These also have index tabs that stick up, but they are placed in between the sub-sections of files. For example, AB, AC, AD.

Files titles These are placed on the right hand side of each individual file.

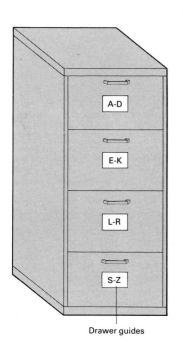

Drawer guides

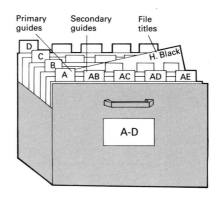

Primary guides   Secondary guides   File titles

The numerical method

With numerical filing each file is given a number and is then placed in the filing system in numerical order. For example, file 1012 would be placed after file 1011 and before file 1013. Guide cards divide the files into groups of ten.

A. Whitcomb	1011
P. Eustace	1012
M. Adams	1013

The main advantage of numerical filing is that it can be easily expanded and this is why many large filing systems use this method.

A disadvantage of the numerical system is that it is not always possible to go directly to the file in the cabinet. Sometimes, an alphabetical index has to be used to find the number given to the file:

Adams, M.	1013
Bath, T.,	86
Cooper, H.,	971
Cullen, V.,	622
Eustace, P.	1012

However, if the appropriate file numbers are quoted on all correspondence it is easy to find the correct file when a letter is received.

The alpha-numerical system combines the alphabetical and numerical methods. The files are divided into alphabetical sections and then each file is given a number within each section. For example, a filing section will contain folders of people whose surnames begin with A. Each folder will then be given a number which will be entered on a guide card together with the folder's title. The guide card will have an index tab marked A. When a letter is received from someone called Adams, the clerk can go directly to the 'A' section and look up the appropriate file number on the guide card.

A

	No.		No.
Adams, M.	1013	Armstrong, N.	825
Allen, P.	999	Ash, E.L.	946
Anderson, A.R.	952		
Andrews, S.C.	1025		
Angus, W.T.	871		
Appleby, J.	860		
Appleton, A.	1030		
Archer, P.	901		

A guide card

The geographical method

When the geographical method of filing is used, papers are filed according to their place of origin; this might be the country, county or town. This method is often used by companies involved in selling, where representatives or agents are responsible for specific areas.

Again, this system is still linked to the alphabetical method of filing. For example, files may first be divided into alphabetical county order:

Avon
Bedfordshire
Cheshire
Clwyd
Fife

and then, within each county section, customers may be filed alphabetically:

Fife
Adams, B.
Burt, M.
Davidson, R.
Jordan, A.

The subject method

With subject filing papers are filed according to topics. The subject folders can be arranged numerically or geographically, but they are usually arranged alphabetically.

A person in business might arrange separate folders for topics, such as, insurance, representatives, security, suppliers and transport. They might even use one complete section for a single topic, such as advertising, and include sub-divisions within this section.

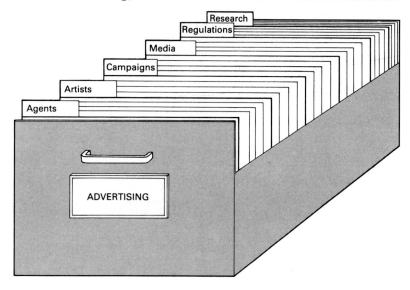

Chronological order

This is quite a complicated sounding name which merely means arranging folders in date order. The more recent papers are kept at the front of the file with older ones to the back.

This method is often used within one of the other systems when papers are kept in chronological order within each folder. This means that the most recent correspondence can be quickly found at the front of the folder. This is important because it is the most recent correspondence that is usually needed.

The chronological system can be used to form a 'follow-up' or 'tickler' system. A file can be set up in chronological order containing details of matters that must be dealt with at some later date. Each day, week or month, the people concerned with the system will look at the file to 'jog' or 'tickle' their memory of some important task they wish to do. Guide cards will divide the days, weeks or months, but usually there are 12 month guide cards and a set of 1-31 day guide cards for the particular month of the moment.

Following is a list of some of the reminders that might be filed in such a system:

- request return of a file borrowed
- important visits to make
- follow-up letter awaiting urgent reply, for example, final request for payment of outstanding account
- plant inspection
- meetings
- holiday rota.

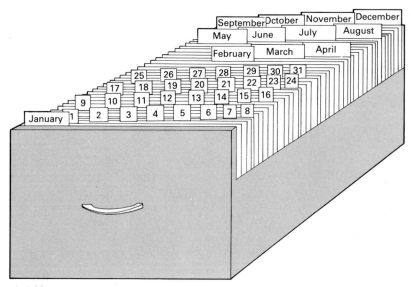

A tickler system

WHAT DO YOU KNOW?

document retention
period
chronological
subject
cross-reference
alpha-numerical
tickler
charging-out
centralised
numerical
alphabetical

Write out all the following sentences filling in the missing words which you can choose from the list at the side of the test.

1 With _____ filing a single department is responsible for all filing.

2 A record of the borrowers of files can be kept in the _____ system.

3 References from one file to another can be made using a _____ card.

4 _____ refers to the length of time documents are kept on file.

5 The _____ system is the most common method of filing.

6 A disadvantage of the _____ system of filing is that it often requires an alphabetical index.

7 The _____ system combines the alphabetical and numerical methods of classification.

8 _____ chron filing means putting papers in date order.

9 A _____ file can be used to jog the memory about an important task which has to be done.

10 With _____ filing papers are filed according to the topics to which they refer.

Answer the following questions by looking back at the text in this chapter.

1 What is filing, and why do we file?

2 What are the essential features of a good filing system?

3 Give an outline of the main arguments for departmental filing.
What do you think are the disadvantages?

4 What is centralised filing?

5 What is the purpose of:
   a out guides
   b cross-reference cards?

6 What is document retention period, and what factors influence its length?

7 Write notes to explain the five methods of classification used in filing. Give examples of when each might be used.

8 With the aid of a simple diagram, explain the purpose of primary and secondary guides.

THINGS TO DO

Your firm has received the following letters on the dates shown in the list. As they were received a number was issued to each letter. Rearrange the order of the list in the following ways:

1 alphabetical order by name
2 chronological order
3 numerical order
4 geographical order by town

Number	Name	Town	Date
112	Tapes Carpets Ltd	Southend	17 June
128	D.C. of Rochford	Thundersley	7 June
132	Mary O'Keefe	Leigh	1 June
129	Tapes Cranes Ltd	Pitsea	19 June
110	John Jones Estates	Canvey Island	16 June
130	Baker of Bankside	Westcliff	8 June
111	N.R. MacAndrews	Glasgow	21 June
127	St. Pancras Station	London	23 June
131	A. Adams	Colchester	1 July
101	Arthur J. Watson & Co.	Cambridge	27 June
113	P. O'Casey	Dublin	25 June
109	Tenby Trading Co. Ltd	St. Helens	18 June
121	C. Baker-Brown	Canvey Island	9 June
114	Adrian Kate Laundry	Rayleigh	28 June
102	A.B. Adams	Hockley	20 June
122	W. MacAngus	Wickford	15 June
103	J. Levy-Johnson	Basildon	6 June
115	4 Ways Printers	Bath	4 June
104	R. McArthur	Loughton	22 June
123	Van Deldon & Co.	Liverpool	10 June
126	5 Star Laundry	Brighton	14 June
124	V. Akar	St. Ives	2 June
106	R. Overton-Smith	Blackpool	24 June
116	4 Star Cafe	Chalkwell	29 June
125	Van Der Beer & Co	Benfleet	26 June
105	David Barron	Canvey Island	13 June
117	A.B.C. Taxis	Southend	5 June
107	Buffers for Books	Rayleigh	30 June
118	De Havilland Engineering	Wickford	11 June
119	Ace Employment Agency	Hockley	2 July
108	D. Barron	Basildon	12 June
120	P. Eustace	Loughton	3 June

12 FILING EQUIPMENT

There is a large variety of filing equipment to choose from, but what you use will depend on:

- what sort of papers you are filing
- how often you need to refer to the files
- the space you have available in your office
- whether you work in a centralised filing department.

Sorting equipment

It is a good idea to sort the papers into piles for each folder before filing, so that it is only necessary to go to each folder once. The concertina type of file can be used for this, although there are a variety of desk sorters available.

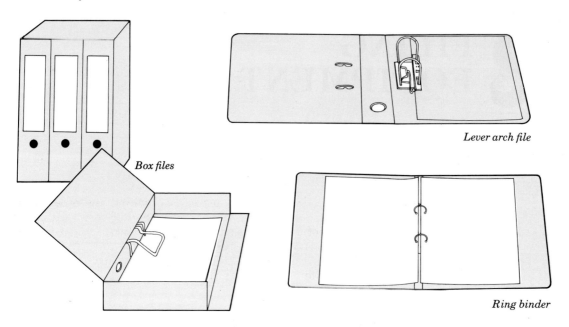

Box files

Lever arch file

Ring binder

Box files

These are box-like containers which are produced in a variety of shapes and sizes. Many are fitted with a thumbhole for easy withdrawal from shelves, and have a large contents label on the spine. Papers are placed in the file and held in position by a spring-loaded arm. These files tend to be used for papers which are not needed very often (for example, previous years' correspondence).

Lever arch files

These files allow papers to be put in or taken out without disturbing those already on file. They have arch-like posts which can be opened by raising a lever. This allows hole-punched papers to be put in order on to the open posts. The arches are then closed by lowering the lever which forms two rings to hold the papers. These files also have a thumbhole and contents label on the spine.

Ring binders

These files are usually smaller than the box and lever arch files and cannot take as many papers. They tend to be used for small collections of special documents, such as price lists. The most common type has two rings, which are opened and closed by a spring mechanism.

Another variation of this file is the thong binder which uses a thread to hold papers in place.

Concertina files

These contain a concertina of indexed pockets into which loose papers can be placed. They are mainly used for temporary storage of documents which are waiting for further attention.

Concertina file

Vertical suspension files

Vertical suspension files are placed one behind the other in a concertina of outer folders, which are suspended from a frame or rail at the top of a drawer in a filing cabinet. Files can be removed from the cabinet without disrupting the outer folders. Each of the outer folders has a clear plastic strip into which can be slipped the title of the file. Usually, these files are kept in a three or four-drawer filing cabinet.

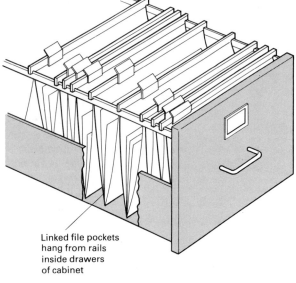

Linked file pockets hang from rails inside drawers of cabinet

Metal cabinets protect documents against fire and vermin

115

Lateral suspension files

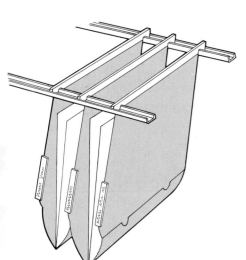

Lateral suspension files are kept in tall cupboard-like cabinets open at both the front and the back to allow the files to be reached from both sides. These files are pocket files suspended from rails fitted across the cabinet, and arranged in rows like books on a shelf. The file titles are put in clear plastic tabs which are fixed to the outer pockets in the vertical position.

Cabinets

We have already examined some of the ways that filing cabinets are used to store documents, but it is helpful to know that they can also be useful in other ways. For example, a number of three-drawer cabinets can be placed together to form a useful worktop, and four-drawer cabinets can be put together to form a screen for a work or reception area.

Rotary decks

There are a wide range of rotary decks which can be used to save storage space in filing. They have a central vertical pillar and the files and pockets are grouped around it. These rotary decks range in size from small decks to hold index cards to larger ones carrying many lever arch or box files. Several people can use these decks at the same time.

A card index drawer

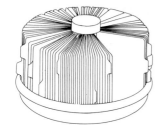

A rotary card index

A wheel card index

Indexes

An index is a good method of filing brief information for quick reference, such as, names, addresses, telephone numbers, numbers of files or book references. A separate card or strip is used for each item, for example, the title of a file or book, or the name and address of a customer. There are two main types of index:

- the card index
- the visible index.

Card index

The card index is the most popular method of indexing and is usually used by libraries, doctors, dentists and opticians. Brief information is filled in on the cards below the card title, and they are then filed. They are usually filed in alphabetical order, in a drawer divided into sections by index cards with sticking-up tabs. Sometimes the cards are filed on a rotary deck or on a 'wheel'.

117

Visible index

This consists of flat trays stored one on top of another in cabinets. Each tray has a number of flaps which can be turned back to show a card on which entries have been made. When the trays are pulled out from the cabinet the title of all the cards are visible at the same time. This is possible because each card sticks out a little further than the one before it. The title of each card is visible through a clear plastic pocket.

Coloured 'signals' can be placed in the title pocket to draw attention to other information. For example, if a business working in sales keeps a visible index of cards containing the names, addresses and buying records of its customers, it can indicate which sales representative is responsible for each customer by using a separate colour code for each salesperson.

If less information needs to be kept, such as, only names, addresses and telephone numbers, it is possible to use a visible strip index. This consists of plastic pockets into which can be fitted strips of card with the required information. This information can then be seen without even having to lift a flap.

Advantages

- They can be referred to quickly.
- They take up little space.

Disadvantages

- The information is limited to the size of the card or strip that is used.

Microfilm filing

The biggest problem of all filing systems is that of storage space, especially for documents that are no longer frequently used. Microfilming has become the ideal answer to this storage problem for firms that can afford it.

Microfilming is a photographic process whereby documents can be photographed and reduced to a much smaller size. Instead of folders full of documents, there are just small rolls of film to store. The original documents can then be destroyed.

The microfilm can be stored in a number of ways, including on roll film, microfiches and aperture cards. When a document is needed the microfilm can be viewed on a scanner or reader unit where the negative is enlarged and projected on to a display screen.

A reader for microfilm

A roll of microfilm

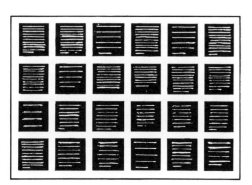

A microfiche is a sheet of film, approximately the size of a postcard, on which many microcopy images have been recorded

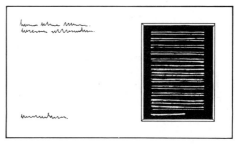

An aperture card can be used to hold an individual piece of microfilm

WHAT DO YOU KNOW?

lateral suspension
worktop
index
microfiche
lever arch
microfilm
rotary decks
signals
vertical suspension
visible strip index

Write out all the following sentences filling in the missing words which you can choose from the list at the side of the test.

1 In _____ files documents are held in position by arch-like posts.

2 _____ files are usually kept in three- or four-drawer filing cabinets.

3 _____ files are suspended from rails fitted across the cabinet and arranged in rows like books on a shelf.

4 A number of three-drawer cabinets can be used to form a _____.

5 _____ can be used to hold index cards.

6 An _____ is a method of filing brief information for quick reference.

7 On a visible index system, coloured _____ can be used to draw attention to special information.

8 A _____ consists of plastic pockets, into which strips of card can be fitted.

9 The main advantage of _____ filing is that it uses so little space.

10 A _____ can be viewed on a reader unit.

Answer the following questions by looking back at the text in this chapter.

1 Why is it advisable to pre-sort documents before filing?

2 Produce three diagrams which will clearly show the difference between box files, lever arch files and ring binders.

3 Explain the difference between vertical and lateral suspension files.

4 Explain the difference between a card index and a visible index. Give examples of when each system might be used.

5 Describe the various equipment used in microfilm filing, and explain the advantage of this form of filing.

THINGS TO DO

Study this plan of a small office. The staff wish to rearrange the layout of the office for a change. They also wish to provide a counter from which to deal with visitors. At the same time they wish to screen off a part of the room from the visitors. They would also like to reposition the coffee machine so that it can be used by both the staff and people waiting at reception.

Draw a new plan showing how you would rearrange the office giving particular attention to more constructive use of filing cabinets.

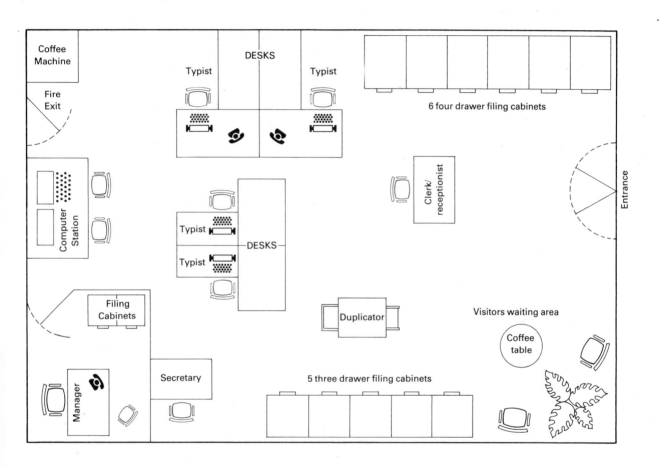

13 MACHINES FOR THE TYPISTS

In recent years the equipment used in offices has become increasingly sophisticated and it is important to keep up with the latest developments. However, the most widely used office machine at present must be the typewriter, and in this chapter we will look at the different varieties available – from the most basic to the most sophisticated.

Typefaces

Typewriter manufacturers produce many styles of type face, including Italic, Gothic and Script. However, the two main typefaces used are Pica and Elite.

```
This is an example of 'Pica' type
which has 10 characters to the
inch (25.4 millimetres).  It is
the most widely used typeface in
business.
```

```
This is an example of 'Elite' type
which has 12 characters to the
inch (25.4 millimetres). This type
gives a smaller print than pica.
```

Standard typewriters

Platen release lever
Carriage-release lever
Line-space regulator
Line-space lever
Tabulation stop clearing key
Margin-release key
Colour change adjuster
Shift lock
Shift keys

Margin stops

Quick feed lever
Paper-release lever
Platen (feed) roller
Tabulator bar
Tabulation setting key
Back-space key
Double spacing selector

Space bar

Standard or manual typewriters depend on power provided by the typist. The typist strikes the keys so that the typeface hits the ribbon and prints the character of the key struck.

Standard machines have the following basic characteristics:

- a standardised keyboard – the keyboard on every machine is set out in the same way
- margin stops
- line space settings for single, double or triple line spacing
- ribbon adjustments, allowing choice of colour print or stencil production.

Modern machine developments have led to excellent alternatives to the standard typewriter, but it still has the following advantages:

- it is cheaper to buy than other typewriters
- it is less expensive to service and repair
- it is not affected by power failures.

Portable typewriters

These machines are designed to be light and easy to carry in a small case. They are usually not strong enough for general office work, although they are used by people who travel in their work, for example, journalists and representatives. They have also become popular for personal use, and it is now possible to buy electric ones.

Electric typewriters

Pressure control

Pitch selection lever

Half back-space lever

Push-variable line spacing

Paper centering guide

Line-space lever

Paper-release lever

Line finder

Left margin stop

Margin-release key

Tabulation control

Right margin stop

Express back-space key

Power on/off switch

Powered carriage return

Automatic repeat spacing bar

Correcting key

These machines have become very popular for use in business. They are run from the main electricity supply, which is used to drive a built-in motor. Even with the lightest touch on the keys they are driven forward to print on the paper.

Advantages

- automatic carriage return and line-spacing
- repeat mechanism on some keys, such as full-stop and underscore (underline)
- even type impression, good appearance
- produces more and better carbon copies
- less tiring for the typist

Disadvantages

- purchase cost is higher than a standard typewriter
- service costs can be more expensive
- a power failure makes the machine unusable

Changing a 'golfball'

One of the more recent developments in electric typewriters has been the production of machines with interchangeable typefaces.

These machines have no typebars. The characters are mounted on a round metal head, sometimes called a 'golfball'. As keys are depressed the machine turns the head so that the correct character strikes the ribbon. The typing head can easily be removed and changed for a different style of type.

Another form of electric typewriter is the automatic, which will produce as many 'original' copies of a letter as required using a program of punched tape or punched cards. These machines are rapidly being replaced by electronic typewriters and word processors.

Electronic typewriters

Traditional type bar and 'golfball' typewriters are rapidly being replaced by electronic machines. In the case of the traditional typewriter each character is linked to a key, and in the case of a 'golfball' machine, each key is linked mechanically to the single element. With an electronic typewriter the link is made through a printed circuit board (microchip). Because the electronic machine has so few moving parts, they are lighter than traditional typewriters, less likely to have mechanical failure, and more easily and quickly repaired.

Electronic typewriters have many useful features:

- Excellent, even quality print.
- Automatic centering (headings automatically placed in the centre).
- Automatic underlining.
- Margin justification — right hand margin can be kept level all the way down, similar to the print in this book.
- Small immediate (resident) memory which can include display of a line of characters allowing amendment and correction prior to print out.
- Long-term memory available with some machines which allows storage of large amounts of text for future use.
- Automatic correction key which can be used to remove characters from the display, and from the paper when using certain types of ribbon.
- Variety of cartridge/cassette ribbons which are easily replaced.

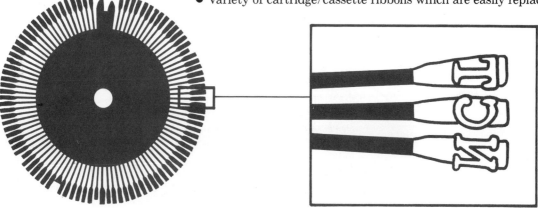

A daisy wheel from an electronic typewriter

A floppy disk

Word processors

One of the most startling recent developments in typewriters has been the development of the word processor. The most basic word processor, the editing typewriter, automatically records what the operator types on a tape or floppy disk, and this information can be displayed on a small television-like screen or visual display unit (VDU).

All word processors have a small amount of internal memory, but this memory can be extended by a variety of storage methods. The most common form of information storage used today is the floppy disk (diskette), which can hold between 80 and 130 pages of A4 text. Material can be located on the disks in seconds.

The typist can correct, alter or rearrange the text until they have built up the 'picture' they wish to print, and they can even justify the margins if necessary. The disk will then be run through taking in all the changes that the operator has programmed. Similar to the automatic typewriter, the word processor will type out however many top copies are required and then the programmed disk can be stored for future use or amendment.

A word processor has a keyboard, a screen (VDU), a central processing unit (CPU), a means of storage (for example, a floppy disk) and a printer

Visual display unit

Keyboard

Line printer

Disk drive

Central processing unit

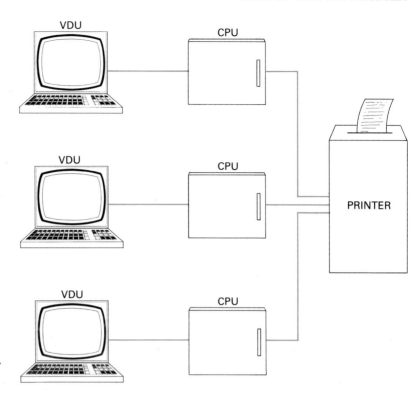

Several operators can share one printer
(This is called shared resources)

Even the word processor is not the end of the story, voice recognition machines are being developed. When fully developed these machines will recognise the spoken word and print direct from dictation.

Care of the typewriter

Taking care of your typewriter is very important. If your machine is going to give good results and have a long life then you must:

- Keep your machine free from dust. Place the cover in position when the machine is not in use.
- When typing always use a backing sheet to protect the platen.
- Always move the carriage to one side when rubbing out, so that the dust does not go into the machine.
- Clean regularly, preferably daily, but at least once a week. Always clean before and after cutting a stencil.
- Only use recommended cleaning equipment.
- Treat the machine with care, many parts are delicate.
- When carrying the typewriter make sure:
  - **a** the carriage is locked
  - **b** the back of the machine is nearest to you
  - **c** you lift the machine using the frame, avoiding finger contact with delicate parts under the machine
  - **d** you never lift the machine by the carriage.

Dictating machines

One of the problems for the business person who employs a shorthand typist, is that both of them must be available at the same time if the boss wishes to dictate a letter. If, however, the business person uses a dictating machine, they can dictate a letter while their typist is doing something else.

Dictating machines are machines which record messages on belts, discs, magnetic spool tape or cassettes, it all depends on the type of machine. The portable machines are especially popular as they allow the executives to dictate their letters where and when they want to, for example, on a train journey, or at home.

The dictator of the letter speaks into the microphone and the machine records the message. The message can be replayed aloud to the dictator and corrected if necessary. The completed dictation is then passed to the typist (called an audio typist) who has a special machine for listening to what has been recorded. They also have a foot control pedal which is used to move the recording forwards or backwards. For example, should the dictation be too fast for the typist to keep up with, they can depress the pedal which takes the recording back to the place that they had reached in their typing. The typist listens to the dictation through a pair of headphones which keeps the recording private.

Advantages

- The typist does not have to be present when dictation is taking place.
- The executive can dictate a letter when it is most convenient to him or her.
- Portable machines make it possible for dictation to be recorded anywhere.
- Work can be more easily shared between several executives and typists.

Disadvantages

- The typist can feel a loss of personal contact with his or her boss.
- Listening through headphones for long periods of time can make the typist feel isolated from colleagues.
- Power failures make the machine unusable.

WHAT DO YOU KNOW?

pica
electronic
'golfball'
floppy disk
dictating
word processor
elite
electric
margin
standard

Write out all the following sentences filling in the missing words which you can choose from the list at the side of the test.

1 _____ type has 10 characters to the inch (25.4 millimetres).

2 The _____ typeface has 12 characters to the inch (25.4 millimetres).

3 The _____ typewriter depends on power provided by the typist.

4 _____ typewriters are less tiring for the typist.

5 A _____ is a form of interchangeable typeface.

6 _____ justification keeps the right hand margin level all the way down.

7 The _____ typewriter has so few moving parts it is less likely to have mechanical failure.

8 A _____ is a means of storing information for the word processor.

9 With a _____ the typist can rearrange the text of a letter.

10 One of the advantages of the _____ machine is that the typist does not have to be present when dictating takes place.

Answer the following questions by looking back at the text in this chapter.

1 Explain the difference between the following pairs:
 a standard typewriter and portable typewriter
 b electric typewriter and electronic typewriter

2 What is the purpose of a 'golfball' in relation to typewriting?

3 What is a 'daisy wheel' and how is it similar to the 'golfball'?

4 What advantages do word processors have over other forms of typewriter?

5 In relation to word processors explain each of the following terms:
 a keyboard
 b Visual Display Unit (VDU)
 c floppy disk

6 You have had a school leaver join your firm. Write them a list of maintenance instructions for care of the typewriter.

7 Explain the work of an audio typist, including a detailed description of the equipment he or she uses.

8 What are the advantages and disadvantages of dictating machines?

THINGS TO DO

1 Several of the typists in your office have come to you and said they are worried about the intended introduction of a word processor. Give an outline of the arguments you would put forward to convince them that the word processor will make their work easier and more interesting.

2 Look at the What do you know? test on page 129. Imagine that we want to move question number 3 to the position following number 10, and then re-number all the questions. Explain how this could be done easily with a word processor, perhaps using simple diagrams to clarify your explanation.

14 REPROGRAPHIC EQUIPMENT

The word reprographic may well be new to you but reprography is the process by which a number of copies can be reproduced from a master copy. The master copy can be an original document, a stencil or an art master and can be typed, written or electronically produced.

In some firms the responsibility for copying is given to a central reprographic department or resource centre. Alternatively, the various copying equipment may be distributed around the firm.

Carbon copying

Carbon paper has a dull side and a glossy side. The glossy side is placed against the paper on which the copy is to be made, and another sheet of paper is placed on top of the dull side. The combined sheets can now be written or typed on to produce a top and carbon copy.

About four copies can be obtained in this manner from a manual typewriter, but an electric machine can produce as many as twenty. When several carbon copies are produced it is called manifolding.

Making up sets of paper and carbon can take a long time. However, this problem is partly solved by the use of stationery sets which have the paper and carbon sheets already together. This system is particularly useful in producing invoice sets when many sets can be joined together to form continuous stationery.

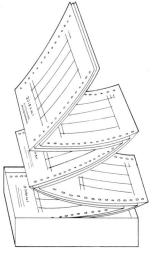

Continuous stationery

Another type of stationery set uses NCR (No Carbon Required) paper, which gets rid of carbon paper entirely. The NCR paper is treated on the reverse side with an invisible carbon coating and on the face side with a reacting agent. When the two surfaces are put together information can be written or typed on the top surface and copied on the one beneath. If several sheets of NCR paper are used, then several copies are made.

The main disadvantage of carbon copies is the limit on the number of copies that can be produced at one time. If a large number of copies are needed other methods of copying must be used.

Stencil duplicating

Stencil duplicating works by forcing ink through impressions cut into a stencil on to a piece of paper beneath.

The stencil

Most stencils are made from a thin wax-like material, although other materials are sometimes used. Stencils can vary in size and quality and which type of stencil you use depends on what you want to produce.

Cutting the stencil

A stencil can be cut in a number of ways. The four most popular ways are:

- by using a stylus
- by using a typewriter
- by using a thermal heat copier
- by using an electronic stencil scanner.

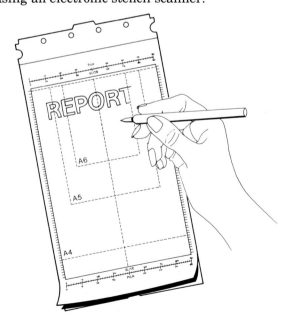

When a typewriter is used to cut a stencil, you:

— Clean the typeface of the typewriter with a stiff brush. You also may need to clean it during the cutting of the stencil.
— Put the stencil into the typewriter with the wax-like side facing you and the stencil heading at the top.
— Switch the typewriter to the stencil production position. Never type a stencil through the ribbon.
— Remember, duplicated copies can only be as good as the master they are produced from. Switch the typewriter to maximum pressure and type with a firm sharp touch to make a clear cut.

When stencils are cut by a thermal heat copier infra-red heat is used to cut them copying from an original document which is passed through the machine.

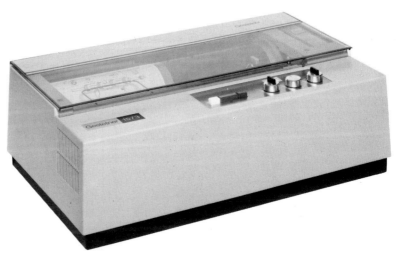

An electronic stencil scanner

Another way to cut stencils by using heat is by an electronic stencil scanner. This machine produces high quality stencils from originals, even including photographs. The original document is placed on a cylinder in the machine, alongside a special stencil. As the cylinder rotates, a photo-electric cell scans the original document and burns the stencil with a series of minute holes to produce a pattern similar to the original.

Correcting a stencil

Mistakes can easily be corrected on a stencil by using correction fluid. This is painted over the mistakes and hardens to form a new surface. This area can now be re-cut with the correct letters. While corrections are being made a plastic ruler should be put behind the stencil to keep it away from the backing sheet until the correction fluid has dried. Always check the stencil before duplicating from it.

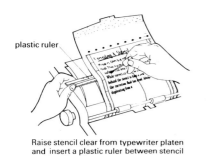

plastic ruler

Raise stencil clear from typewriter platen and insert a plastic ruler between stencil and backing sheet.

Stencil printing

The prepared stencil is fastened around a cylinder on the duplicator. This cylinder contains ink and has a porous pad on the outside. As the cylinder is rotated the ink is fed through it. The ink then passes through the impressions which have been cut on the stencil on to the duplicating paper. This reproduces the image that was cut into the stencil. One ink stencil can produce up to 7,000 good copies, depending on the quality of the stencil.

Stencil duplicating machines can be electrically and manually operated. The electric machines are more expensive than the manual ones, but they can automatically produce 150 copies a minute, feeding fresh paper into the machine from one side and stacking printed copies on the other. Every stencil duplicating machine has a numbering device to count the numbers of copies printed, and the electric machine will automatically stop when the required number of copies have been produced.

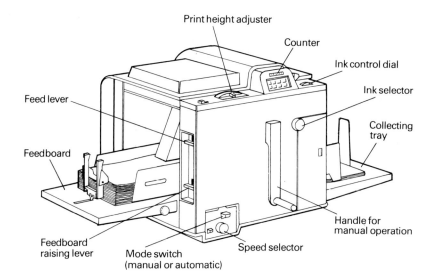

A stencil duplicator

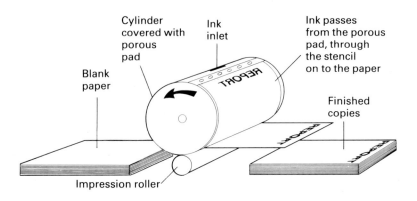

Storing stencils

Stencils may be stored and used again when required. Surplus ink is blotted off the used stencil with duplicating paper while the ink is still wet. Then the stencil is dried to make sure that the backing sheet does not get stuck to it. When the stencil is dry it should be stored either flat or suspended in a stencil storage cabinet.

Spirit duplicating

Spirit duplicating produces copies from a master copy which is a sheet of special art paper. This art paper is white and one side of it is shiny. This is then backed with a special carbon paper, called hectograph carbon paper, which also has a shiny side.

Making the master copy

— The shiny sides of the art paper and carbon paper are put so that they face each other. This means that whatever is typed or written on the topside of the art paper, will appear as a mirror image on the under side.
— When typing a spirit master it is not necessary to switch the typewriter to stencil, but it is necessary to type evenly and firmly to produce a clear image. A special hard backing sheet is available to help produce a good even deposit of carbon on the art paper when it is being handwritten.
— The hectograph carbons come in different colours and by changing the carbon and keeping the same master copy a multi-coloured master can be produced.
— Masters can also be made by using a heat copying machine.

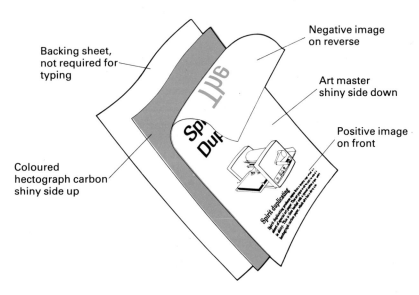

Backing sheet, not required for typing

Negative image on reverse

Art master shiny side down

Positive image on front

Coloured hectograph carbon shiny side up

The printing process

— The finished master copy is fixed on to the cylinder of the spirit duplicator.
— This cylinder then rotates and comes into contact with the copy paper which has been fed into the machine.
— **The duplicating paper is moistered with spirit by a pad before caning into contact with the master copy.**
— As a result of the spirit a little of the carbon comes off the master on to each sheet of copy paper and an image is produced.
— As each sheet takes a little carbon from the master, eventually, there is not enough carbon left to produce any more copies.
— The master then has to be thrown away.

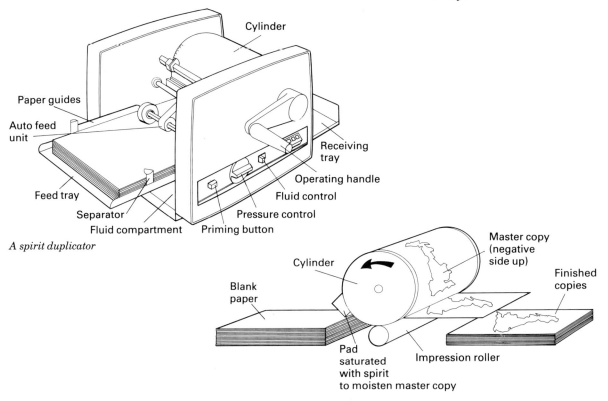

A spirit duplicator

Advantages

- It can produce multi-coloured copies.
- It is economical for short runs.
- It is simple to operate.
- It is particularly good for producing diagrams.
- There are manual and electric machines available.

Disadvantages

- It has a maximum limit of 300 good copies.
- The print tends to fade if left in the light for a long time.
- The spirit catches fire easily and therefore it needs special storage.

Offset litho duplicating

Although the duplicators outlined so far can be used to produce varied and attractive copies, the quality of reproduction can never be as good as the quality of printed matter. The offset litho process, however, can produce this high quality.

Offset masters

Offset litho duplicating involves producing a master copy which has a greasy image of the information that is going to be reproduced.

The master copy is called a plate and is usually prepared on either paper or metal. A paper plate has a life of between 2,000 and 5,000 copies, but a metal plate can produce between 20,000 and 50,000 copies. How many copies a metal plate actually does produce depends on its quality.

Making the plate

This can be made by several methods:

- typing, using a lithographic (greasy) ribbon
- writing, using pens with special oil-based inks
- electronic scanners
- photocopiers, heat copiers.

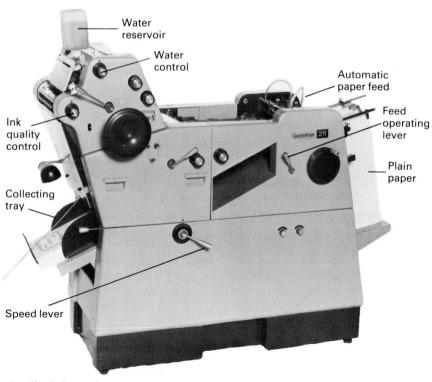

An offset litho machine

The offset process

Remember, the offset process depends upon the fact that grease and water will not mix.

— The plate is fitted to the plate cylinder with the positive image facing away from the cylinder.
— Next, moisture is automatically applied to the plate. The moisture will only wet the background and not the greasy image on the plate, because the water and grease will not mix.
— Rollers now ink the plate with a greasy ink. Because the water and grease will not mix only the image is inked.
— The plate then comes into contact with the rubber cover of the offset cylinder and a mirror (negative) impression of the inked image is made on it.
— Then, as paper is passed between the offset cylinder and the impression cylinder, the image is reversed again and a positive impression is made on the paper.

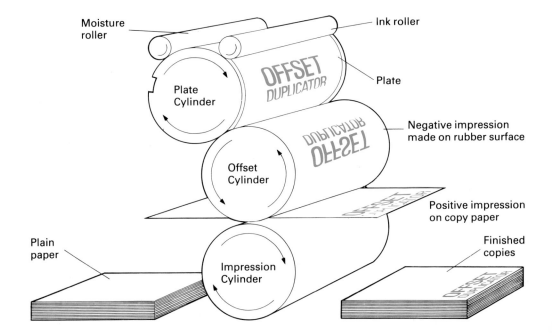

Advantages

- The quality of reproduction is high.
- It will reproduce typewriting, drawings and photographs.
- It is economomical for long runs.
- The plates can be stored and then used again.

Disadvantages

- The machine is expensive when compared to other duplicators.
- It is uneconomical for short runs.

Office photocopiers

Office photocopiers make exact copies of original documents. Photocopying is a quick method of making a copy of an original document. The old method of photocopying relied on exposure of a sensitive paper on which a negative copy of an original was made. This negative was fed back into the machine and positive copies were produced. This method relied on the use of wet chemicals which was inconvenient and messy. The development of 'dry copiers' has largely got rid of liquid operated 'wet' copiers.

Dry copiers may be: dyeline, thermal, dual-spectrum or electrostatic copiers.

Dyeline copiers

There are two stages in this process of producing copies:

Stage 1

— The original document is placed on top of a sheet of yellow, diazo-coated paper (paper coated with diazo salts).
— The document and the diazo paper are then exposed to ultra-violet light.
— The diazo paper is bleached white, except for the places beneath the type and the lines of the document. These remain yellow.

Stage 2

— The diazo paper is passed through a developer which develops and darkens the yellow print. This makes a positive image appear.

Thermal copiers

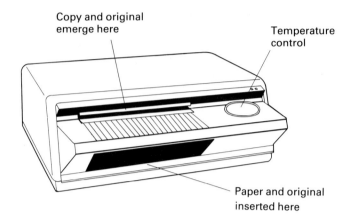

Copy and original emerge here

Temperature control

Paper and original inserted here

These machines produce copies by using infra-red heat.

Copying process

— The original document is fed through the machine with a sheet of special heat-sensitive paper.
— Any type or writing on the document which has used a carbon-based ink absorbs the infra-red heat rays and warms up.
— This in turn acts upon the heat sensitive paper and produces a copy of the original.

Advantages

● The thermal copiers are small.
● They are easy to use.
● They are cheap to run.
● They can also be used to make spirit duplicator masters, ink stencils and overhead projector transparencies.

Disadvantages

● They will only copy a document if it has been typed or written with carbon-based ink.

Dual spectrum copiers

There are two stages to this process of producing copies:

Stage 1

— Ultra-violet light rays are used to produce a negative image of the original document while it is being passed through the machine. This negative image is invisible.

Stage 2

— The sheet of paper with the negative image is then fed through the machine again to produce a thermal copy of the original. This copy has a positive image.

Because these machines use ultra-violet light they can copy any original, even if the print does not have a carbon base.

Electrostatic copiers

These copiers have been one of the major developments in recent years. The basic principle of these machines is that they use the force of static electricity to produce a copy of a document.

There are a great many different types of machines which use the above principle, but some of the main characteristics are as follows:

— There are two electrostatic processes: the xerography process and the electrofax process. Machines which use the xerography process copy on to plain paper, while those which use the electrofax process require specially coated paper.
— There are machines into which the original is fed in sheet form and kept in the machine until the required number of copies have been produced. Other machines copy from single sheets or pages of books which are laid on a flat bed and not fed into the machine.

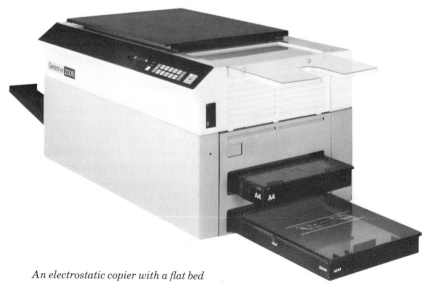

An electrostatic copier with a flat bed

The original is fed into this electrostatic copier and is kept in the machine until the required number of copies have been produced

— Most electrostatic machines have a selection mechanism which allows us to set the number of copies required of an original. Some machines will have automatic document feeder equipment. This will take a pile of sheets of originals and automatically feed them in one at a time, as well as produce the required number of copies. A sorting device can be attached to some machines to allow the collating (sorting into order) of copies. For example, it will sort a selection of copies into order ready for stapling into booklets.

Advantages

- These machines are fast.
- They are easy to operate.
- The reproduction is of excellent quality.
- Long runs are possible automatically.
- They will copy photographs.
- Copies do not fade.
- They can copy pages from intact books.
- Some machines can produce plates for offset duplicating.

Disadvantages

- They are expensive to buy or hire.
- Skilled servicing is required.

Collating machines

Collating means putting sheets of paper into order and collecting into sets. Imagine you have duplicated ten different pages of a report and they now need to be put into order and stapled together. How would you organise this?

The most likely method you would choose is to spread the piles of the different pages around a large table in the sequence of the report. You, or a clerk, would then work around the table picking up each of the sheets in turn, stapling them together when you had collated each copy of the report.

Collating machines makes this boring and tiring exercise unnecessary because they will automatically make up sets of documents. There are many different kinds of collating machine, but a basic principle is that there is several trays into which are placed piles of numbered sheets. These piles of sheets are obviously placed in correct order so that when the machine is switched on it will select the sheets one at a time, stack them in sets and even staple them together.

WHAT DO YOU KNOW?

thermal
dry
stencil
reprography
spirit
collating
dual spectrum
clean
NCR
offset litho

Write out all the following sentences filling in the missing words which you can choose from the list at the side of the test.

1 _____ is the process by which a number of copies can be reproduced from a master copy.

2 _____ paper produces copies without the use of carbon paper.

3 _____ duplicating works by forcing ink through impressions cut into a thin wax-like material on to a piece of paper beneath.

4 When cutting a stencil by using a typewriter, always _____ the type before you begin.

5 The _____ duplicator can produce multi-coloured copies.

6 The _____ duplicating process is based on the principle that water and grease will not mix.

7 Dyeline, thermal, dual-spectrum and electrostatic copiers are all _____ copiers.

8 A _____ copier uses infra-red heat to produce copies of an original document.

9 Ultra-violet light is used by the _____ copier to produce a negative.

10 Sheets can easily be collected into sets using a _____ machine.

Answer the following questions by looking back at the text in this chapter.

1 Compare carbon paper with NCR paper.

2 With the aid of simple diagrams explain how to produce a stencil for duplicating. Also show how to correct a mistake on a stencil.

3 Produce a labelled diagram to show how the stencil duplicator works.

4 Explain how to produce a master and duplicate with a spirit duplicator.

5 Copy and explain the diagrams which illustrate how the offset litho duplicator works.

6 Write brief notes to explain the use of the various types of office copier.

7 What are the disadvantages and the advantages of electrostatic copiers?

8 Explain the manual method of collating a booklet and show how the collating machine makes this task easier.

THINGS TO DO

1 Towards the end of your course arrange for each person in your class to complete a different 'missing words' test from this book. The whole test should be written or typed on a spirit master or stencil master, with the answers underlined. Sufficient copies of each test should be printed so that everyone in the class has a copy of each of the tests for revision.

2 Draw and label diagrams of both the stencil and spirit duplicators. Obtain a paragraph of print from each machine to include with your notes.

15 DATA PROCESSING MACHINES

Much of the work of an office involves the creating, storing, retreiving and processing of various kinds of information, and sending information from one place to another. In recent years a number of machines have come into use to assist with these information processing tasks. The most important of these machines are adding machines, calculating machines and computers.

Information in a form which can be stored and processed on a machine, particularly a computer, is known as data. The machines which work with the information are given the name of data processing machines.

Adding machines

A large amount of the data processing that is carried out in offices involves straightforward adding and subtracting. This can easily be carried out by the adding or add-listing machine.

The adding machine can be manually or electrically operated. It has a simple keyboard allowing adding and subtracting of figures, and keys are available for producing totals and sub-totals. These machines are not able to divide and they cannot multiply. For example, 4×2 will be entered into the machine as $2+2+2+2$.

Some machines have a roll of paper (called a tally roll) on which all information is printed as the machine deals with it. When the machine has a tally roll it is called an add-listing machine.

Calculating machines

A desk calculator

At one time calculating machines were operated manually. Nowadays, however, electrically or battery driven calculators containing silicon chips have become so cheap that they have taken the place of the manual machines.

An electronic calculator not only adds and subtracts in the way that an adding machine does, but it also multiplies, divides and stores information. How much information it is able to store depends on the type of machine. The calculating machine is also fast, silent and the data results are shown in an illuminated panel.

Computers

The most important development in data processing machines has been the computer. Computers were originally designed for scientific and engineering purposes, but their use very soon spread to offices. Computers are now used for a wide variety of office tasks, and their numbers in offices are increasing very rapidly. They are bringing about big changes in office organisation. The office which does not have a computer is becoming increasingly rare.

Computers carry out five types of operations:

- *Accepting data from a user* This operation, known as input, is most commonly carried out by typing the data on a keyboard similar to a typewriter keyboard.
- *Supplying data to a user* This operation is known as output, and generally takes the form of printing the data, or displaying it on a screen similar to a television screen.
- *Processing data* This can involve sorting or selecting the data, performing calculations or making simple decisions based on the data.

- *Storing and retrieving data*   All computers have a memory, which stores the data they are processing at any time. Computers also have permanent methods of storing data. The most common storage medium is floppy disks, which are flexible disks on which the data is stored in a magnetic code.
- *Communicating data*   Most modern computers can send and receive data to and from other computers, or computer terminals which are devices for the input and output of data. Data communications can be over a short distance, to other computers in the same office, or over long distances, using telephone or satellite links.

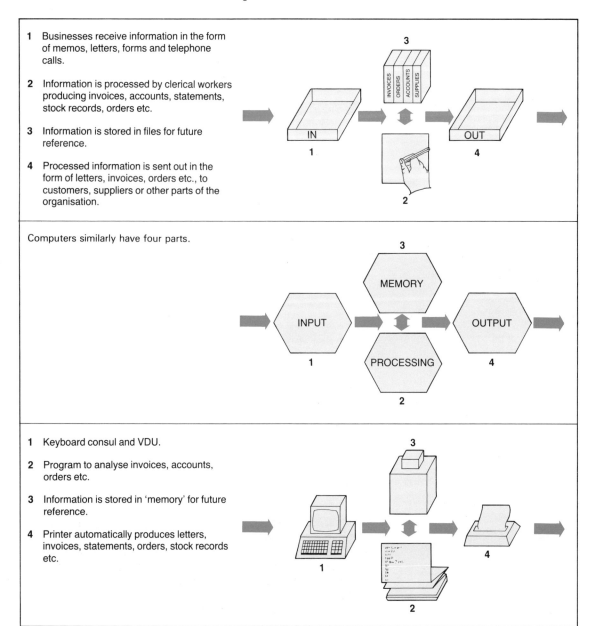

1 Businesses receive information in the form of memos, letters, forms and telephone calls.

2 Information is processed by clerical workers producing invoices, accounts, statements, stock records, orders etc.

3 Information is stored in files for future reference.

4 Processed information is sent out in the form of letters, invoices, orders etc., to customers, suppliers or other parts of the organisation.

Computers similarly have four parts.

1 Keyboard consul and VDU.

2 Program to analyse invoices, accounts, orders etc.

3 Information is stored in 'memory' for future reference.

4 Printer automatically produces letters, invoices, statements, orders, stock records etc.

Computers carry out their data processing operations in response to sets of instructions called programs. Programs are generally stored on floppy disks and loaded into the computer memory when required. The programs for most office computers are supplied with the computer. All that the person using the computer has to do is call up the program required for the task and set it running.

The parts of the computer which carry out the processing of the data, and form the computer memory, are called chips. Chips are made mostly of silicon, are very small and contain no moving parts. They work very fast, using small pulses of electricity for their operation. Many small computers do all their processing on a single chip, called a microprocessor. The high speed, reliability and ever decreasing cost of chips is one of the main reasons for the great increase in the number of computers in use.

A microchip

Visual display unit

Line printer

Disk drive

Keyboard

Floppy disk

Boxmore County Council Libraries

0 084064 01

Reader's name B. Green

Address 13 Linley Gardens, Hightown

*This library card shows a bar code. The
code is 'read' using a light pen*

The world of computers is one of rapid change. Cheaper, faster,
more powerful and easier-to-use computers are becoming available all the time. Better methods of input and output are
constantly being devised. For a number of years, the commonest
media for data input were punched cards and paper tape, but
today, most data is entered directly at the keyboard, or read from
bar codes using special readers. Printing is used less and less for
output – modern visual display screens have sophisticated
graphics (pictorial representation) facilities, often in colour. If a
hard (printed) copy of output is required, it is often placed directly
on microfilm.

Some common computer terms

Bar codes	Reference code numbers incorporated in bar-coded labels containing a pattern of vertical lines. Used to identify library books or price and stock number of supermarket products. The code can only be read by a special device such as a light pen, and the information is fed to the computer.
Data	Information in a form which may be stored and processed by a computer.
Datel	The service provided by British Telecom for the transmission of data between computers, using the telephone network.
Hardware	The physical components making up a computer.
Program	A set of instructions which makes a computer carry out a particular task.
Software	Another word for program.
Terminal	A device, containing a keyboard and printer or screen, connected to a computer, and used for the input and output of data.
Visual Display Unit (VDU)	A terminal at which output is displayed on a television-like screen.

Chips are changing the office

Computers are being used for a wide variety of office tasks, and
further applications are being introduced all the time. The use of
computers has made it necessary for many office workers to be
retrained, in order to learn the skills required to operate the new
equipment.

Some of the most important tasks of office computers are word
processing, accounting, payroll preparation, stock control and
management information systems. These are outlined overleaf.

Word processing (see Chapter 13)

Specially adapted computers, called word processors, are replacing typewriters in many offices. Documents are typed on a word processor in exactly the same way as on an ordinary typewriter, but they are stored on floppy disks instead of being printed directly on paper. The documents may also be displayed on a VDU, corrected or changed, combined with other documents or transmitted to another word processor, as well as being printed.

Accounting

Firms need to record the value of goods sold to customers and to keep up-to-date information on how much each customer owes them. All this information can be fed into a computer and stored on a floppy disk so that a record is maintained of each customer's trading position with the firm. Invoices and statements of accounts are printed by the computer, and warning notices can be produced automatically when a payment is late.

Advanced accounting systems allow transactions to be carried out by a direct link between the computers of the two companies concerned.

Payroll preparation (see Chapter 17)

The majority of companies produce their weekly or monthly payroll by computer. Records are kept on floppy disks of the payroll details of each employee, and variable data, such as hours worked, sickness and overtime, is entered before each payroll run. The computer may even print payslips and cheques, or arrange for the direct transfer of salaries into employees' bank accounts.

Stock control (see Chapter 16)

In companies which have warehouses, computers are used extensively for stock control. Records are kept of the stock levels of all items, and often of their locations in the warehouse. Movements of goods into and out of the warehouse are entered into the computer, which prints all the paperwork required, and can even re-order goods automatically when stock levels fall below the minimum.

Small stock control programs are sometimes used for supplies such as office stationery and furniture.

Management information systems

Managers of modern companies have an urgent need for concise, accurate and up-to-date information about all aspects of their company's operation. A variety of management information programs are available for office computers. These programs can examine large files and print or display summaries of relevant information, and enable managers to forecast the consequences of current trends, or various decisions they are required to make.

WHAT DO YOU KNOW?

store
floppy disk
hardware
output
data
input
add-listing machine
memory
program
VDU

Write out all the following sentences filling in the missing words which you can choose from the list at the side of the test.

1 Information which can be stored and processed on a machine is known as _____ .

2 An _____ is an adding machine which has a tally-roll.

3 Some calculators can _____ information.

4 The information a computer accepts is known as _____ .

5 _____ refers to data supplied by a computer to the user.

6 The computer's _____ stores information.

7 The _____ is the most common storage medium used with computers.

8 The _____ is the set of instructions given to a computer.

9 The physical components of a computer are known as _____ .

10 Computer input and output can be displayed on a _____.

Answer the following questions by looking back at the text in this chapter.

1 Briefly explain the five types of operation performed by computers.

2 'Chips' have revolutionised computers. What are 'chips'?

3 Explain each of the following terms:
   a hardware
   b program
   c software
   d terminal

4 Choose three traditional office jobs and explain how computers have changed them. Include a brief description of the jobs and skills that may become redundant and the new skills that office workers will be required to learn.

THINGS TO DO

1 **a** Each published book has its own individual identity, or ISBN, number. Find the ISBN of this book.

   b If each book and each library ticket holder have their own bar code identities, find out how a library can use this information to keep an accurate record of all books borrowed and returned.

2 Items being totalled up at a supermarket check out also show a bar code. This code can include the price of the product and a stock item number. Find out how this type of coding can:

   a Make it easier to work out the total value of each person's purchase.

   b Help to keep computerised records of stocks up to date.

3 Following are some further activities in which computers are used. Choose two of these to investigate further to produce a specific description of the way in which computers can be used.

   Police work, airline reservations, premium bonds, insurance, calculation and payment of wages, bank records.

16 STOCK RECORDS

'Stock' is the term used to describe the items which a business holds in a stockroom, or some other special place, for future use. This stock may take many forms:

- it may be goods on shop shelves awaiting resale
- it may be raw materials in the factory warehouse waiting to be manufactured into finished goods
- it may be the internal stationery supply for the office.

Whatever the stock is to be used for, it is important to the business because it represents a part of the capital (value) of the business.

A business will keep a record of the stock it has for several reasons:

- for security purposes
- so that at any time it can tell the quantity and value of the stock held
- to make sure that the amount of stock held does not fall either too low or rise too high.

Minimum stock

The business will decide a minimum level that it will allow the stock of each item to fall to. When the stock level reaches this minimum level, the company will order further supplies or production. When these new supplies are received they are added on to the stock record. As orders are supplied to customers they are subtracted from the stock record. The minimum stock figure is important because it helps to avoid running out of stock.

It is important that the business does not run out of stock because:

- it might lose an order it would have gained
- it could lose future business because the customer goes to someone else for supplies and is satisfied with the new supplier.

The minimum stock level is worked out in the following way:

— how much stock is used a week (say 100)
— how long it takes for new stock to arrive (say 5 weeks)
— allow one week extra (total 6 weeks)
— $6 \times 100 = 600 =$ minimum stock level

Maximum stock

A simple answer to the problem of running out of stock could be to say, 'Always keep a large amount of goods in stock at all times.' But this is not usually a sensible answer for the good business person because the more money they have tied up in unnecessary stock, the less profitable their business is likely to be.

A wise business person will set a maximum stock level to make sure that they are not tying up too much of their capital. There are no clear cut rules for deciding on a maximum stock level, but it will be influenced by:

- the advantage of quantity discounts to be obtained by placing bulk orders
- the desire to keep down the amount of capital tied up in stock.

Stock keeping tips

- Avoid running out of stock.
- Do not carry more stock than necessary.
- Run the business with as little capital 'sitting on the shelves' as possible.

Keeping stock records

On the stock record card below, it will be seen that the record shows an initial stock and that each customer's order is deducted from the stock as it is dealt with. When the stock falls to the minimum level new production or supplies are ordered. When the new stock arrives it is added to the existing stock. Each calculation will result in a new balance.

STOCK RECORD CARD

Item: Child's Shoe - Article 3480
Stock Price: £7.20
Location: Warehouse 3

Max. Stock: 10,000
Min. Stock: 5,000

Size	1	2	3	4	Total
Initial Stock	2000	3000	3000	1000	9000
Smith 1/11/83	100	200	200	100	600
	1900	2800	2800	900	8400
Jones 7/11/83	50	100	100	50	300
	1850	2700	2700	850	8100
Harris 12/11/83	675	1325	1395	625	4020
	1175	1375	1305	225	4080
Production 13/11/83	700	2000	2000	300	5000
	1875	3375	3305	525	9080

Obviously, if a mistake is made in one of the deductions or additions the stock record becomes worthless. It is quite simple to check for mistakes by cross-checking the figures. This is done by adding across the columns to make sure that they add up to the figure shown in the total column.

Many firms will have a code or stock reference number for each item in stock. The stock reference number is useful because it can:

- save the trouble of entering a full description of the stock
- help to distinguish between items with a similar description
- help in computerised handling of stock data
- make it possible to file stock cards in numerical order for easy reference.

An alternative style of stock card is shown below. This type of stock card is basically divided into two halves, one to record goods received (receipts) and the other to record stock being taken out (issues).

This particular stock card records stock used within the company. In other words it refers to supplies of stocks to departments within the firm and not to supplying customer's orders. You should note, that when items are taken out of the internal stock, a requisition number is shown and not an order number. This makes it easy to see whether an order comes from within the firm or from a customer.

INTERNAL STOCK
STATIONERY STOCK CARD

Item: Paper A4 White - 23086   Maximum stock: 100 Reams

Location: Room 37   Minimum stock: 30 Reams

DATE	RECEIPTS			ISSUES			BALANCE IN STOCK
1983	Supplier	Order No.	Quantity	Department	Req. No.	Quantity	
7/4/83							90
8/4/83				Sales	134	20	70
9/4/83				Pool	139	20	50
12/4/83				Buying	146	20	30
12/4/83	J.Roberts	12266	70				100
14/4/83				Export	149	20	80
16/4/83				Accounts	153	50	30
16/4/83	J.Roberts	12357	60				90

Column to show date record was altered   Columns where new stock is recorded and added   Columns where outgoing stock is recorded and subtracted   Column to show changing balance

Remember

- When new supplies are received into the stock they are entered in the receipts column and added to the balance column. The order number which goes with the new stock is also recorded.
- When supplies are given to other departments they are recorded in the issues column and subtracted from the balance column.

When one stock card is full, a new one will be started. The new stock card will obviously begin with the same stock figures that the previous stock card ended with.

Stocktaking

Annual stocktaking

Annual stocktaking or inventory is carried out at the end of the firm's financial year to establish the value of the goods in stock. This can take a long time and involves physically checking that the goods stated on the record are present. The value of the stock is calculated by multiplying the number of items present by either the cost price or current selling price, whichever is the lowest.

For example if the stock contains 100 reams of typing paper, cost price £1-50 per ream, then the value of the paper is $100 \times £1\text{-}50 = £150$.

This will be done for each of the items held on stock and the value of all the stocks are added together to form a closing stock value. This figure is shown in the final accounts for the year.

Perpetual inventory stocktaking

A disadvantage of annual stocktaking is that because it is only carried out once a year, any stock shortages or pilferage (stealing) are only discovered once a year.

The continuous stocktaking or perpetual inventory overcomes this difficulty. A team of specialist stocktakers are employed to make periodic stock checks on a few items at a time and without any warning to the storekeepers.

WHAT DO YOU KNOW?

minimum stock
stock reference number
added
inventory
capital
subtracted
maximum stock
perpetual inventory stocktaking
requisitions
closing stock value

Write out all the following sentences filling in the missing words which you can choose from the list at the side of the test.

1 Stock represents a part of the _____ of a business.

2 Stock will be allowed to fall to the _____ level.

3 The _____ level can make sure that a business does not tie up too much capital in stock.

4 A _____ helps to distinguish between items with a similar description.

5 _____ are requests for supplies from within the company.

6 Receipts into stock are _____ to the stock figure.

7 Issues are _____ from the stock figure.

8 _____ is another name for annual stocktaking.

9 The total value of stock is called _____.

10 In _____ a team of specialist stocktakers are employed to make periodic stock checks on a few items at a time.

Answer the following questions by looking back at the text in this chapter.

1 What is stock and why is it important to a business?

2 What points must be taken into account when deciding on a maximum stock level?

3 Copy the stock record on page 155, and explain the method and purpose of cross-checking.

4 What is the purpose of a stock reference number?

5 What is the purpose of an annual inventory and how is it carried out? What is the advantage of perpetual inventory stocktaking?

6 How is closing stock value calculated, and what is the purpose of this figure?

THINGS TO DO

1 Draw up a blank internal stationery stock card similar to that shown in this chapter. Complete the stock card for A5 plain white paper using the following information.

Stock at June 11 198_ was 90 reams

June 12 issued 20 reams to art department, requisition no. 110
June 13 issued 30 reams to sales department, requisition no. 118
June 15 received 300 reams from Key Office Supplies, order no. G1079
June 17 issued 60 reams to accounts department, requisition no. 123
June 20 issued 30 reams to typing pool, requisition no. 130

Maximum stock 500 reams
Minimum stock 50 reams

This stock is stored in Room 50

2 On the reverse of your stock card:
   a Explain the difference between an order and a requisition.
   b What is the purpose of fixing a minimum stock level?

17 WAGES

Wages and salaries can be looked on as 'the payment in return for work', which is paid to the employee by the employer. The 1960 Payment of Wages Act stated that wages may be paid by legal tender (notes or coins), by cheque or credit transfer.

The term wages is generally used if a person is paid on a weekly basis. If a person is paid monthly, then the term salary is used.

The calculation of wages

Flat rate

This is a set rate of pay per week or month which does not alter, however hard or otherwise, the employee works. In respect of an office worker this would be their standard rate of pay, and the employer would expect them to give a little more time and effort at busy times without expecting extra payment. At the same time, during periods when there is less work to do the employee would not expect to receive a reduction in pay.

Time rate

This rate means that a worker receives a set amount for each hour worked, or in other words, a fixed rate of pay per hour. If a worker is late for work, the amount of time lost is calculated to the nearest quarter of the hourly rate and will be deducted from their pay.

When an employee is paid at a time rate, they will have a time card (clock card) which is kept in a rack near a time clock. As the employee arrives and leaves work they 'clock' on and off. The time card is put into the time clock and the time is printed on to it. The wages clerk will then use the time card to calculate the employee's wages.

If an employee is asked to work late they are paid overtime for the extra hours worked. When overtime is worked the rate of pay is higher than normal.

Piece rate

One of the difficulties with time rate is that there is little incentive (reward) for the hard-working employee. Many firms, especially manufacturing ones, overcome this problem by also offering a piece rate. When an employee is also paid by piece rate it means that they are paid a certain amount for each item produced or job completed. The more they produce the more they earn.

When this rate is being paid it is important to check the quality of the work being produced or job being carried out. This is often checked by people known as quality controllers. These controllers make sure that any work below a certain standard is returned to the employee who produced it. This means that the employee is only paid for work of good quality.

Bonus

This is another system of rewarding employees for increased output and hard work. The employer finds out the average time it takes to do each job. Then, if an employee, or group of employees, is able to do the job in less than this time, they are paid a bonus. The value of the time saved is divided equally between the employer and the employee. For example:

rate of pay per hour	=	£4-00
average time for job	=	2 hours
actual time taken	=	$1\frac{1}{2}$ hours
time saved	=	$\frac{1}{2}$ an hour
50% of $\frac{1}{2}$ an hour	=	$\frac{1}{4}$ of 1 hour pay
a $\frac{1}{4}$ of 1 hour's pay	=	£1-00
£1-00	=	bonus received

Commission

Many people who are in the selling side of a business work for a commission. This means that every time they sell an item they are paid a percentage of its selling price. Therefore, the more items the sales person sells, the more they earn. Some sales people work on a commission only basis, but others may receive a small salary as well.

Deductions from wages

Statutory deductions

These deductions are payments, enforced by law, that have to be deducted from wages and salaries.

Remember

- Gross pay refers to an employee's wages before any deductions have been made.
- Net pay is the amount left after the deductions have been made.

Income tax

Total TAXABLE PAY to date	Total TAX DUE to date
£	£
1081	324·30
1082	324·60
1083	324·90
1084	325·20
1085	325·50
1086	325·80
1087	326·10
1088	326·40
1089	326·70
1090	327·00

All wage earners are liable to pay income tax and the amount they pay depends on their earnings and their personal circumstances. People pay income tax to the Government through the Department of Inland Revenue.

Most wage earners pay their income tax through a system called PAYE (pay as you earn). The income tax year runs from 6th April to 5th April, and during the year the employee pays some of their yearly tax bill each time they are paid. The amount of income tax to be paid each week is found out by the employer by referring to tax tables and the employee's code number. Both the tables and the code number are supplied by the Department of Inland Revenue.

Every employee on PAYE is given a code number which shows the amount of income that they are allowed to earn before they begin to pay any income tax. In other words, the code number shows their tax-free pay. The higher the code, the greater is the tax-free allowance. A code number is given to an employee after they have filled in a Claim for Allowance form. This form has to be sent to the Inspector of Taxes. The amount of tax-free allowance that they receive will depend on their responsibilities and commitments.

For example:

Personal allowance – each taxpayer is allowed a certain amount, although how much they receive depends on whether they are married or single.

Dependent relative allowance – if a taxpayer looks after an aged parent or other relative they receive an allowance.

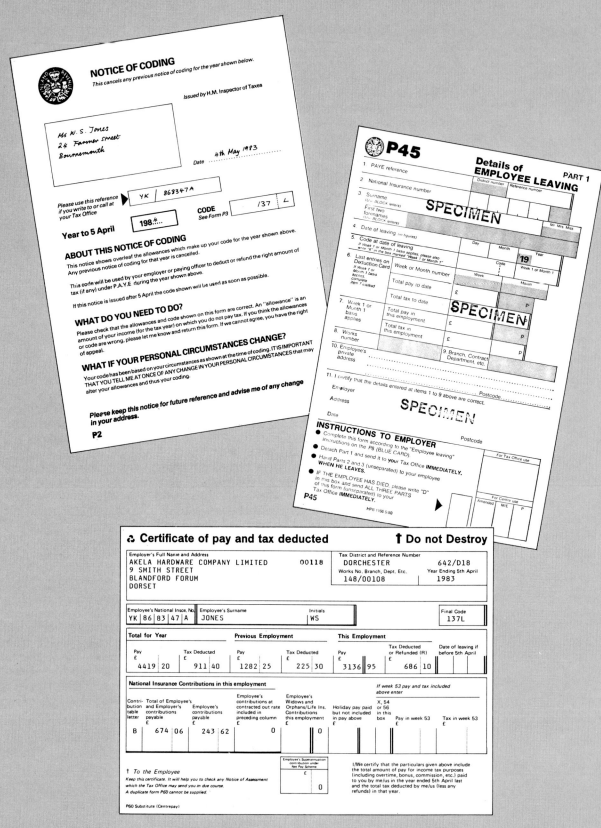

Expenses to do with a job – an allowance is given if a taxpayer has to buy special clothing or tools for their job, or if they have union fees to pay.

A notice of coding (form P2) is sent to every wage earner before each new tax year. This tells them their code number and how it has been calculated. If the taxpayer feels that their code is unfair they have time to object before any payment becomes due.

If an employee changes their job during the income tax year, their employer gives them a P45 form. This form states their code number, their year's earnings to date and the amount of income tax so far deducted. The new employer is then given this form so that they can continue their new employee's income tax payments at the correct rate.

At the end of each tax year the employer gives the employee a P60 form, which is the yearly 'certificate of tax deducted'. The P60 states how much the employee has earned during the tax year and how much income tax has been deducted.

National Insurance

National Insurance is another deduction from wages which must be paid by all working people over the school leaving age, unless their earnings are below a certain amount.

Each working person is given their own 'National Insurance number' by the Department of Health and Social Security, and the money they pay to this State-run scheme is recorded against this number. Contributions are collected on behalf of the Government by employers and forwarded to the Collector of Taxes. The amount that each person pays depends on how much they earn.

Contributions to the scheme:

- A certain amount is given by the employee. This is a percentage of their gross pay.
- A certain amount is given by the employer. This is also a percentage of the employee's gross pay.

The percentage rates of the contributions are reviewed each year.

Benefits available under this scheme include:

- retirement, widows and invalidity pensions
- unemployment benefit
- sickness benefit
- industrial injury benefit
- maternity benefit
- child allowance
- guardian's allowance
- death grant.

If National Insurance payments are not made regularly by an employee, it can mean that the benefits will be reduced if claimed.

Voluntary deductions

Some firms will offer schemes which the employee may also join if they wish, such as private pension schemes, sports and social clubs, and savings schemes. If an employee joins any of these schemes the extra amounts will also be deducted from their gross pay.

One such voluntary deduction which the employee might choose is SAYE (Save As You Earn). This is a Government-run savings scheme where wage earners contract to have an amount regularly deducted as savings from their earnings over an agreed number of years.

Payment of wages

Whether payment of wages is made by cash, cheque or credit transfer, the employee receives a pay advice. This may be a slip of paper or details printed on a pay packet containing cash.

The wages department fill in the pay advice so that the employee can see how their net pay has been reached. A typical pay advice will show the following information:

- employee's name and work number
- tax code
- National Insurance number
- gross pay
- bonus/commission/overtime
- deductions – National Insurance, income tax, etc.
- net pay.

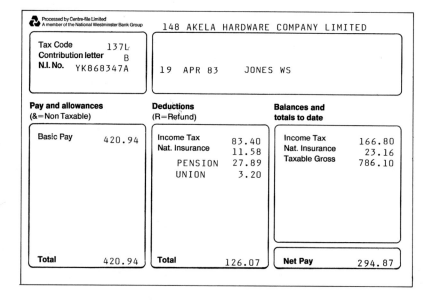

Processed by Centre-file Limited
A member of the National Westminster Bank Group

148 AKELA HARDWARE COMPANY LIMITED

Tax Code   137L
Contribution letter   B
N.I. No.   YK868347A

19 APR 83   JONES WS

Pay and allowances (&=Non Taxable)		Deductions (R=Refund)		Balances and totals to date	
Basic Pay	420.94	Income Tax	83.40	Income Tax	166.80
		Nat. Insurance	11.58	Nat. Insurance	23.16
		PENSION	27.89	Taxable Gross	786.10
		UNION	3.20		
Total	420.94	Total	126.07	Net Pay	294.87

WHAT DO YOU KNOW?

salary
bonus
P45 form
pay advice
wages
notice of coding
flat rate
legal tender
overtime
PAYE

Write out all the following sentences filling in the missing words which you can choose from the list at the side of the test.

1 _____ and salaries can be looked at as 'the payment in return for work'.

2 Notes and coins are _____.

3 The term _____ is used to refer to the monthly payment of earnings.

4 _____ is a set rate of pay.

5 A time rate worker will be paid _____ when working extra hours.

6 The value of a _____ is divided equally between the employer and the employee.

7 Most wage earners today pay their income tax through the _____ system.

8 The _____ tells a worker their tax code for the forthcoming year.

9 The _____ tells an employer the tax position of a new employee.

10 A _____ tells the employee how his net pay figure has been calculated.

Answer the following questions by looking back at the text in this chapter.

1 Briefly explain each of the following methods of payment:
 a flat rate
 b time rate and overtime
 c piece rate
 d bonus
 e commission

2 How does the employer establish how much income tax must be paid by the employee?

3 What is the purpose of the tax code? On what basis is the code established?

4 Explain the purpose of the P45 form.

5 What is National Insurance and who contributes to this scheme? What benefits are available to people who make regular payments?

6 What is the purpose of a pay advice and what information is it likely to show?

7 Explain the difference between PAYE and SAYE.

165

THINGS TO DO

1 Look again at Chapter 2 and the section which describes flexible working time. Give a brief description of the way in which the use of time cards and time clocks could be helpful when workers are on flexitime.

2 You are the wages clerk of a large manufacturing company and one of your jobs is to complete time cards. Employees are allowed five minutes when clocking in or out. If they are more than five minutes late, they lose half an how's pay.

   a Copy Paul Stone's time card, filling in all the details given below. Then work out the total hours for: basic hours worked, overtime worked, and Saturday hours worked. Use the following details:
   — Paul Stone's rate of pay is £3-00 per hour for a 5-day, 40-hour week.
   — Overtime is paid at the rate of time and a half for evening work and double time for Saturday work.
   — Normal hours of work are 0800 to 1700, with a lunch break from 1200 to 1300 hours.

   b Calculate the total gross wage of Paul Stone for this week.

   c Wages are sometimes paid in cash. Name two other methods by which Paul Stone might be paid his wages.

   d From his gross pay certain statutory deductions will have to be made. What are they?

   e Name two possible voluntary deductions from wages.

TIME CARD

Works No	Department	Employee's Name	Week Commencing
384	Goods Inwards	Paul Stone	Mon. 10.12.1983

Day	Ordinary Time				Overtime		Hours		
	In	Out	In	Out	In	Out	Basic	Overtime	Saturday
Monday	0758	1200	1257	1700	1730	1930			
Tuesday	0800	1202	1300	1702					
Wednesday	0802	1201	1302	1703	1730	1932			
Thursday	0806	1200	1301	1700					
Friday	0759	1202	1259	1701					
Saturday					0759	1202			
					Total Hours				

...... hours at £ ...... = ...

...... hours at £ ...... = ...

...... hours at £ ...... = ...

Total gross pay £ _____

18 REFERENCE BOOKS

The office worker who knows the answer to all the questions that arise during their work may be impossible to find. However, a knowledge of how to use up-to-date reference books helps to answer many of the queries which arise.

Most businesses will have a collection of useful reference books for general use in the office, although the content of the collection will depend on the size of the firm and the type of business they are in.

General reference books

Dictionaries

Not only does a good dictionary show you how to spell a word, but it also shows you the pronounciation (how to say it). It also shows you the plural of the word, which language it comes from (its origin) and what part of speech it is (i.e. noun, verb, adjective).

Ready-reckoners

Pocket calculators have largely replaced these books. However, they are still useful as they provide tables for making instant calculations.

Roget's Thesaurus of English Words and Phrases

This book contains a collection of English words and phrases which are arranged in groups according to their meaning. The word in question is looked up in the index. This word will show a number which refers to the section in the book in which the word can be found, along with a list of synonyms (words of similar meaning) and sometimes a list of antonyms (words with opposite meanings).

Pear's Cyclopaedia

Published yearly, this is a small version of the full volumes of encyclopaedia. It provides information on world events, important people, law, central government, foreign phrases, first aid hints, gardening, cookery and various other everyday information.

Whitaker's Almanack

This is an annual publication which gives worldwide information and statistics on subjects such as the governments of countries, political structures, population, languages and international trade. It also gives facts such as tide tables and religious calendars, and more detailed information about Britain, covering government, the Law, education, insurance and many other subjects.

Atlases

These are books which show maps of different countries, continents and the world. Good atlases will show political and population features as well as geographical facts.

Election registers

Available from local councils, these registers list the names and addresses of all persons who are able to vote within the area covered by the register. These registers are useful to people in business if they want to check the name and address of someone, or if they want to carry out market research surveys.

Hansard

This book provides a record of the actual words spoken in parliamentary debates.

Communication reference books

Telephone directories

These are supplied to subscribers by British Telecom, together with dialling instructions and STD code books. These, together with the classified trade directories (yellow pages), are important office reference books (see Chapter 5 for details).

The Post Office Guide

This reference book is essential to any business. It is issued every year by the Post Office and published by Her Majesty's Stationery Office. It gives information on all postal services offered by the Post Office, including charges and regulations related to inland and overseas post, savings, investment and money transfer services.

Charges shown in the Guide are quite often changed and the Post Office, therefore, issues free supplements about every two months. These corrected sheets can then be stuck into the Guide over the out-of-date pages.

Telex directories

These list the call number of subscribers to the telex service.

Travel reference books

Motoring handbooks

Available from the A.A. and the R.A.C., these handbooks give useful information about roads, routes, garages, restaurants and hotels. These are essential when planning a journey, particularly when private transport is used.

A.B.C. Guides

A.B.C. Railway Guide This is published monthly and gives details of all railways services to and from London, including information about destination towns, such as early closing days for shops, population and main hotels.

A.B.C. World Airways Guide This guide is also published monthly, and gives details of scheduled air services throughout the world. Fares, freight rates, travel agents and the different countries' visa requirements are also shown.

A.B.C. Shipping Guide This is also published every month, and gives such information as, shipping line services, ports, dates of sailing, fares and ferry services.

A–Z Street Guides

These are detailed street maps of different towns. These guides also show the numbering direction of buildings in each street, as well as giving details of places of public interest. An alphabetical index of streets make these maps easy to follow.

Miscellaneous reference books

The following reference books offer information about important people, professional bodies and the armed services. They are not kept in all offices, but they may be found in most libraries.

Trade association publications

Most of the major trades have a trade association or professional body which represents their members. These associations will often try to establish codes of practice for their members and will deal with enquiries regarding the trade. The journals which many of these associations publish are useful references for those in the same trade.

Who's Who

This book gives a variety of information about important and famous people who are alive. *Who was Who* gives similar information about people who are dead. Other books about important people are: *Debrett's Peerage and Titles of Courtesy, International Who's Who*, and *Who's Who in America*.

Crockford's Clerical Dictionary

This book gives details of church people and their organisations.

The Medical Directory, The Dentist's Register, The Register of Nurses

These books provide information about the medical professions and their services.

The Army List, The Navy List and The Air Force List

These books provide information about officers of the armed services.

The Law List

This book gives information about members of the legal profession, such as solicitors, barristers and judges.

Trade Associations and Professional Bodies of the UK

This book gives the addresses and telephone numbers of important trade, professional and technical associations in the United Kingdom.

WHAT DO YOU KNOW?

telex directories
Roget's Thesaurus
yellow pages
Post Office Guide
ABC Guides
motoring handbooks
ready reckoner
Who's Who
dictionary
Whitaker's Almanack

Write out all the following sentences filling in the missing words which you can choose from the list at the side of the test.

1 A _____ is used to find the spelling of a difficult word.

2 Instant calculations can be made using a _____.

3 _____ can be used to find words of similar meaning.

4 Details of population, production and revenue of foreign countries can be found in _____.

5 The name, address and telephone number of a local builder may be found in the _____.

6 _____ list the call numbers of subscribers to the telex service.

7 The _____ gives full details of the services offered by the Post Office.

8 _____ contain useful information about roads, routes, garages and hotels.

9 The _____ provide details of rail, air and shipping services.

10 _____ provides a variety of information about prominent people who are still alive.

Answer the following questions by looking back at the text in this chapter.

1 List the following reference books and beside each one write a brief explanation of the information which can be found in it:

 a Pear's Cyclopaedia
 b Whitaker's Almanack
 c Trade associations' publications
 d Roget's Thesaurus

2 What information can be found in the Post Office Guide? How can you make sure your copy is always up to date?

3 Which reference books would you use to plan a journey to a foreign country? Give reasons for your choice.

4 What sort of people would you expect to find listed in the following reference books?
 a Crockford's Clerical Directory
 b The Medical Directory
 c The Army List
 d The Law List

THINGS TO DO

1 Rearrange the following list of reference books so that they correctly pair up with the description of the information they contain.

A dictionary	Information about famous people
Election registers	Details of travel services
Who's Who	A record of the actual words spoken in parliamentary debates
The A.B.C. Guides	Names and addresses of people entitled to vote
Hansard	The spelling and pronounciation of words

2 Refer to your 'yellow pages' directory and list six businesses which can provide each of the following goods and services:

carpets   life assurance   house painting   tropical fish
plumbing   removals   scrap metal   typewriters

EXAMINATION REVISION

Having worked through this book you may now be preparing for your examinations and may want to test your knowledge of the subject. The following tests are based on the contents of the book, and all the answers can be found in the text. However, you should first test your knowledge without looking back through the book.

True or false?

Look at each of the following statements and decide which are 'true' and which are 'false'.

1 A credit note is used to correct an undercharge.
2 R.D. written on a cheque means 'return to drawer'.
3 A current account is one that keeps changing.
4 The person who writes out a cheque is called the drawer.
5 Confravision is operated by the Post Office.
6 A routing slip is used to direct a visitor round the firm.
7 The Telex Service provides immediate transfer of printed messages.
8 P.A.Y.E. is a method of paying National Insurance contributions.
9 Recorded Delivery is the best way to send jewellery by post.
10 When documents are filed according to topic this is called subject filing.
11 A company's teleprinter code number can be found in the Telex Directory.
12 Poundage refers to the weight of a parcel.
13 A machine which prints postage on envelopes is called a franking machine.
14 If an advertisement for a job asks you to write in the 'first instance' you should write the letter of application by hand.
15 The marginal sign N.P. means 'start a new page'.
16 To make regular payments you should apply to the bank for a standing order form.
17 A cheque becomes out of date when it is three months old.
18 A cheque received by post is called 'post dated'.
19 If you draw more money out of the bank than you have in, this is called an overdraft.
20 When an employee leaves his job he is given a P45.
21 Inter-departmental correspondence is often in the form of a memorandum.
22 The system whereby tax is deducted from earned income is called S.A.Y.E.
23 The letters 'E & OE' on an invoice reserve the right to correct an error at a later date.
24 Pica type is larger than Elite type.
25 A stencil for use in duplication is best drawn using a stylus.

26 Hectograph carbons are used for spirit duplicator masters.
27 The Telex Service uses teleprinters.
28 A statement of account would show prices of the individual goods.
29 Cash discount is offered to encourage the buyer to pay promptly.
30 If a trader buys goods for £300 less 25% trade discount, they would pay £150.
31 A consignment note is sent with goods transported by a carrier other than the seller's own vehicle.
32 VAT must be charged on all invoices.
33 A credit note is usually printed in red.
34 It is not necessary to issue a receipt when payment has been made by cheque.
35 Trade discount is normally allowed by traders if an account is settled within a stated period.
36 A cheque crossed with the name of a particular bank is an example of a special crossing.
37 Interest is normally paid on a deposit account.
38 The name given to the person a cheque is written out to pay, is the drawee.
39 An office collating machine is used for dispensing coffee and tea.
40 Your income tax code number is based on the allowances to which you are entitled.

Short answer questions

Each of the following questions should be answered in one sentence.

1 Where would you find a list of local plumbers and their telephone numbers?
2 Which duplicator can produce several colours at the same time?
3 Under which letter of the alphabet would you file correspondence from '4-Ways Printing Company'?
4 State two compulsory deductions from pay.
5 In an advertisement for a job you see the words 'L.V.s provided'. What are 'L.V.s'?
6 What is the name of the British Telecom teleprinter service?
7 Name two methods of communication which might be used by members of the same firm.
8 What information would be shown on form P.60?
9 Name two possible voluntary deductions from pay.
10 Which department of a firm deals with recruitment of staff?
11 What is the name of the system by which most people in Britain pay income tax?
12 Name one advantage of using audio dictating machines.
13 What do the letters 'C.O.D.' stand for?
14 What is the most common storage medium used with computers?
15 What is the purpose of a pro-forma invoice?
16 Which form of typewriter incorporates a V.D.U.?

17 What have we done if we have endorsed a cheque?
18 Which reference book would you refer to for a verbatim report of a parliamentary debate?
19 What is the correct name for the numbers and letters at the end of an address?
20 Give the correct name for the list of items to be discussed at a meeting.
21 Name two recorded telephone services.
22 Which reference book would tell you a company's teleprinter code number?
23 Name three ways wages may be paid.
24 Which form of cheque is safest to send through the post?
25 On which type of bank account do you receive interest?
26 What is the name of the office machine which records telephone messages?
27 Name the Post Office service which is most suitable for delivery of valuables.
28 How many sheets of paper are there in a ream?
29 Which size paper is the larger, 'A4' or 'A5'?
30 Which system of arranging files is most suitable for copies of invoices?
31 Name the machine which marks a postage rate and date on the mail.
32 How would you indicate that something other than the letter is enclosed in an envelope?
33 Which reference book would you refer to for details of postage rates?
34 What is the name of the document which tells the buyer that the goods are on the way to them?
35 Which document would be used when ordering goods.
36 What is the name of the guides which show the main divisions of a filing system?
37 Which machine is most suitable for destroying confidential documents.
38 If you require five copies of a document, which would be the cheapest way to do it?
39 If you are required to draw dotted lines on a stencil, which instrument would you use?
40 If you are travelling a great deal, with no fixed address, which Post Office service would you be likely to use?

Multiple-choice questions

In the following, a statement or question is followed by several possible answers, only one of which is correct. Choose the correct answer.

1 Which document would you send to a customer to summarise their debt for a complete month's transactions?
   a an invoice
   b an advice note
   c a statement of account

2 STD means:
  a subscriber trunk dialling
  b special telephone directory
  c subscriber telephoning direct

3 A telephone answering machine:
  a asks you to call again later
  b records a message
  c tells you the number is no longer connected

4 A telephone credit card:
  a allows you to pay telephone bills monthly
  b is used to make purchases on credit from a shop
  c allows a subscriber to make calls when away and pay later

5 When you pay money into a current account you:
  a use a credit transfer form
  b complete a debit note
  c fill in a credit slip

6 If the words 'a/c payee' are added to the crossing of a cheque, this means:
  a the cheque can only be paid into the account of the payee
  b only the payee can amend the cheque
  c the payee has endorsed the cheque

7 Which of the following would be sent by Recorded Delivery?
  a £50 in notes
  b a set of valuable stamps
  c a final demand for payment of an outstanding debt

8 The following should be sent by Registered Post:
  a a valuable piece of jewellery
  b a cheque in excess of £500
  c a birth certificate

9 Cheques and other payments received in the post should be:
  a entered in a remittance book
  b recorded in the petty cash book
  c acknowledged immediately

10 A 'tickler' system can be used to:
  a record files borrowed
  b indicate cancelled appointments
  c remind people of future matters requiring attention

11 A postage book:
  a is used to record amounts spent on postage
  b holds postage
  c gives current postal rates

12 National Giro is operated by:
  a building societies
  b the commercial banks
  c The Post Office

13 In what book is the expenditure on small items for the office recorded?
  a a petty cash book
  b a remittance book
  c a post book

14 What is the name given to the recorded notes of what took place at a meeting?
a agenda
b minutes
c report

16 An open cheque has:
a no drawer's signature
b the amount omitted
c no crossing

16 An endorsed cheque is one which has been:
a stamped by the bank
b signed by the bank
c signed on the back by the payee

17 Which public corporation is responsible for operating ,the telex service?
a The Post Office
b British Telecom
c The Telex Corporation

18 Who is responsible for the proper conduct of a formal meeting?
a the secretary
b the managing director
c the chairperson

19 The imprest system is used for:
a petty cash
b keeping paper tidy
c filing imprests

20 Which of the following does not incorporate a VDU?
a a teleprinter
b a word processor
c a computer

21 What is the name given to the deduction for prompt payment?
a cash discount
b trade discount
c quantity discount

22 When would you use an out guide card in a filing system?
a when the filing clerk is absent
b to replace a borrowed file
c to indicate a file which can be taken away

23 A cross reference means that:
a a document has been filed under more than one heading
b documents marked X are no longer required
c your boss is unhappy with your work

24 A spirit duplicator is a copying machine requiring:
a a good quality stencil
b hectograph carbon masters
c ink supplies

25 Which reference book would you use to find out a company's teleprinter code number?
  a The Post Office Guide
  b a telex directory
  c an A.B.C. Guide

26 In an advertisement you find the abbreviation C.W.O. What do these letters stand for?
  a credit with order
  b cheque with order
  c cash with order

27 When documents are filed according to topic, this is called:
  a subject filing
  b geographical filing
  c chronological filing

Statements to be completed

Complete the following sentences by filling in the missing words. Choose the words from the lists below.

pool	Yours faithfully	National Insurance
N.C.R.	Teletex	company secretary
ink	certificate of posting	P.M.B.X.
compensation	collating machine	credit card
Bureaufax	primary guides	receptionist
Confravision	geographical	Post Office
debit note	deposit	requisition
alphabetical	Clearing House	stock records
personal	A5	hung
imprest system	poundage	statutory
correcting fluid	business reply service	Roget's Thesaurus
reprographic	drawee	radio
P.A.Y.E.	telephone alphabet	ex-directory
memorandum		

1 An exact copy of a photograph or document can be transmitted instantly by using the _____ service.

2 A switchboard which requires an operator to make all connections between extensions is called a _____.

3 _____ refers to a network which allows visual discussions to take place between groups of people hundreds of miles apart.

4 A _____ corrects an undercharge in an invoice.

5 A _____ is an internal request for supplies from stock.

6 _____ paper is half the size of A4.

7 The _____ arrangement of names is the basis for most filing systems.

8 For business correspondence the complimentary close normally used is _____.

9 A _____ is a machine which saves time when sorting a multi-page booklet.

10 The licence for a franking machine must be obtained from the _____.

11 Suspension filing means that the folders are _____ from rails.

12 The _____ is used to record petty cash.

13 The letters N.I. stand for _____.

14 _____ refers to the charge made by the Post Office for a postal order.

15 The correct name for the department responsible for copying is the _____ department.

16 _____ is a method of paying income tax.

17 A _____ is a form of written inter-departmental communication.

18 _____ refers to someone who is a telephone subscriber, but is not listed in the telephone directory.

19 Income tax is a _____ deduction from wages.

20 A _____ telephone is used for contacting people in cars and boats.

21 No carbon paper is required when making copies using _____ paper.

22 We would find a list of words which could be used instead of 'application' in _____.

23 In a large organisation the executive responsible for dealing with legal matters would be the _____.

24 'Barclaycard' is a type of _____.

25 The purpose of _____ is to direct your eye quickly to the section of files you want.

26 The medium used in stencil duplicating is _____.

27 _____ is used for correcting mistakes on stencils.

28 A _____ proves that a letter has been posted.

29 The Post Office service which enables a firm to obtain replies to letters sent to a customer, without the customer paying the postage, is called _____.

30 A fee is paid to register a packet. This entitles the sender to _____ if the packet is lost.

31 The British Telecom _____ Service enables the business person to send an A4 page of text in less than 10 seconds.

32 The bank on which a cheque is drawn is correctly referred to as the _____.

33 Visitors to a firm are the responsibility of the _____.

34 In a typing _____ a typist generally takes work from a number of different persons.

35 When using the telephone you can spell out difficult words using the _____.

36 Filing under place names is called _____ filing.

37 A _____ telephone call is one for which the charge does not start until the person called is reached.

38 A bank _____ account earns interest.

39 Cheques are settled through the Bankers' _____.

40 When we take an inventory we are checking _____.

INDEX